BAD **FREAKING** ART

BAD FREAKING ART

by noah g freaking thomas
published in 2090

dedicated to mommy, daddy, my husband, my twin
sister Azazael, my mexican pool cleaners Contrero and
Carysa, Gordo Lompkins over at that Denny's down the
way, and of course, asian people: y'all guys really
don't get enough credit

T GALLERY

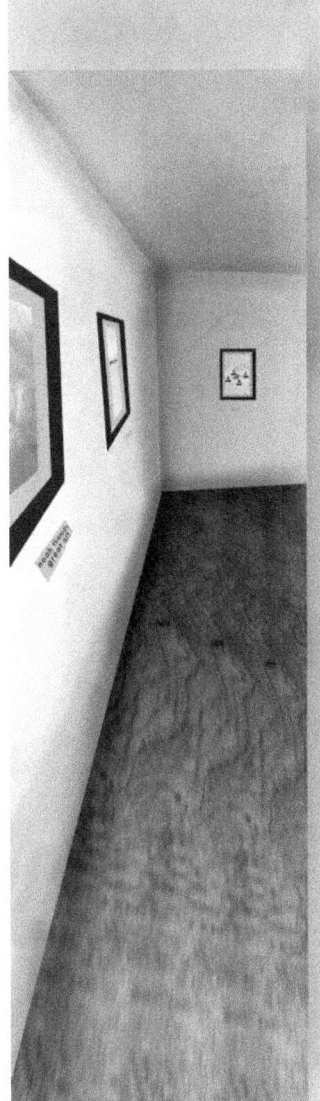

introduckshin

i would like to welcome you to the most best art gallery to ever fit in a 6 by 9 inch paperback

but i'm not with you rn, so i'll have to welcome you over this intro page

so *fricking welcome*

over the next 200 pages of absolutely tortuous frick you're going to feel like you're actually in a real life legit art show with all the fancy freaking rich people and deep meanings and weird furniture and that crap

it's all the fun of going to an art showing without all the judgemental looks from effiminate men with plaid scarves and watermelon martinis

that's right females and gentlemen, now you can enjoy the pleasures of art shows without having to put on pants

just go rn in your room and take off your pants

immediately

do it right now.

thank you please enjoy lol hi mom

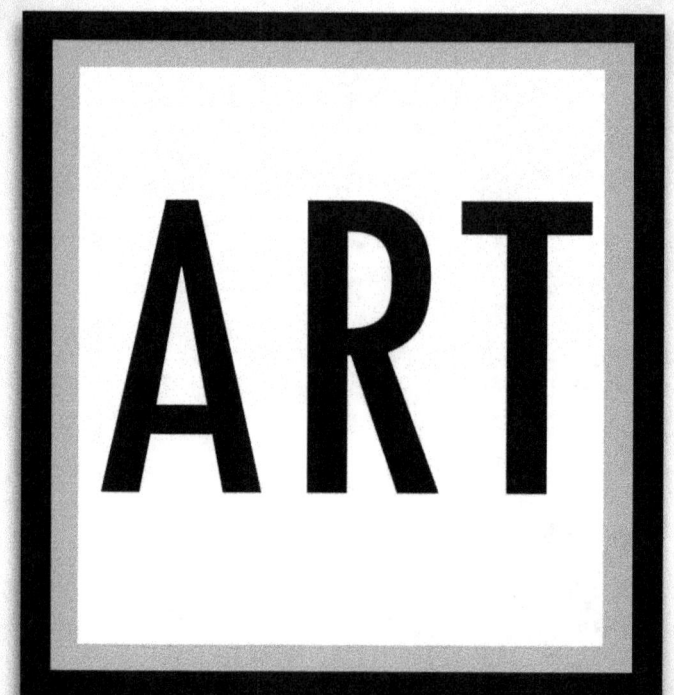

a perfect painting

APT

i did this one wrong

*i couldn't decide what
color i wanted the canvas
of this painting to be*

i fear i am becoming
increasingly indecisive

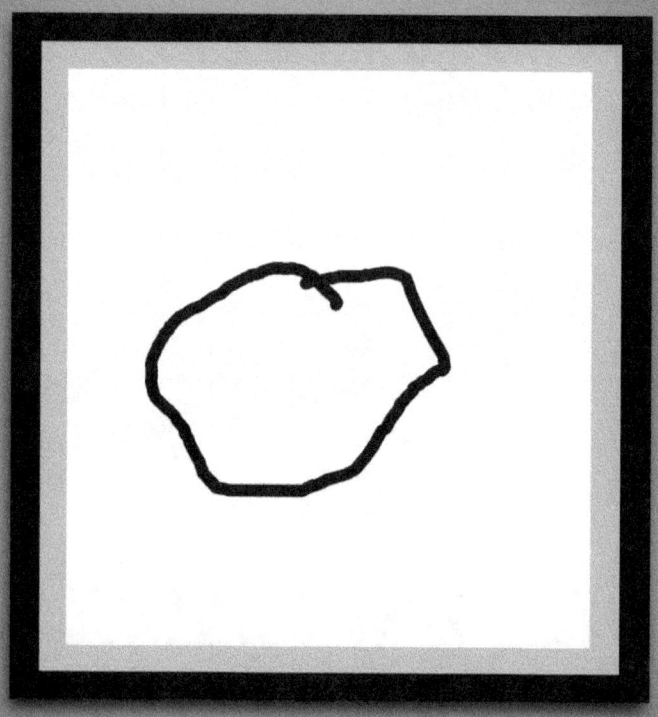

i almost drew a really
good circle here

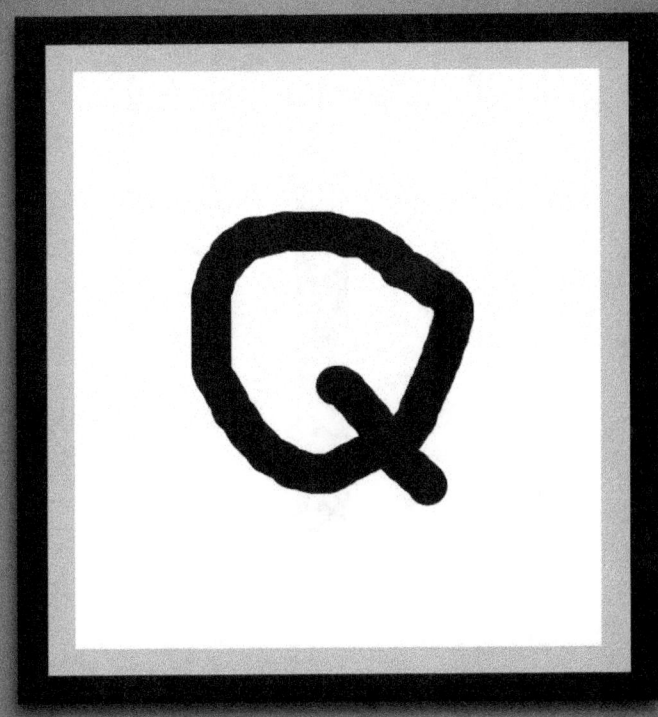

*definitively the best
number*

a melted popsicle stick

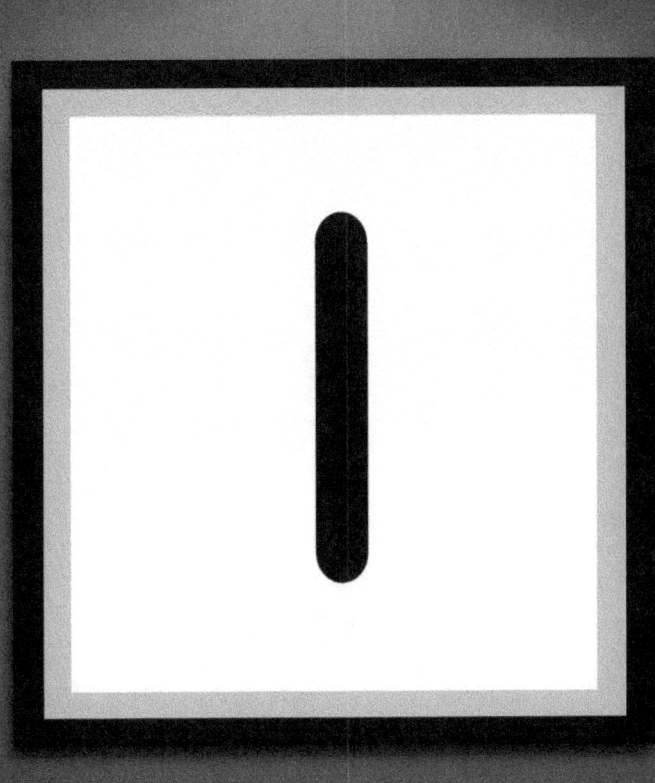

a frozen popsicle stick

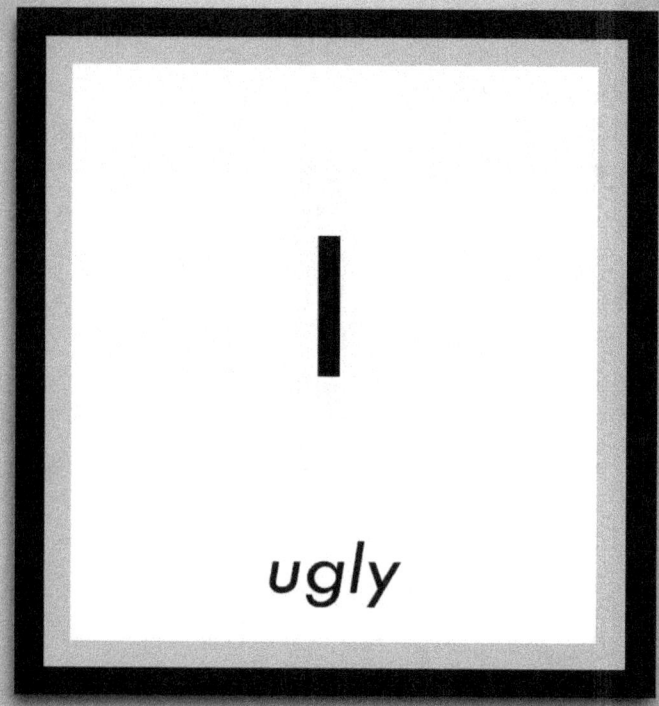

ugly

this is an ugly one

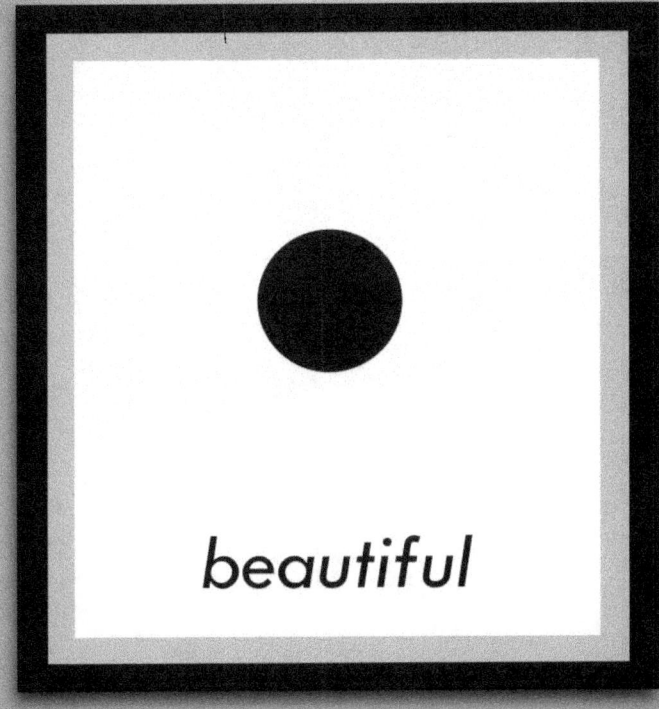

beautiful

on the other hand this
one is beautiful, take that
society

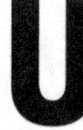

U

neither

title

the name of this of this is john

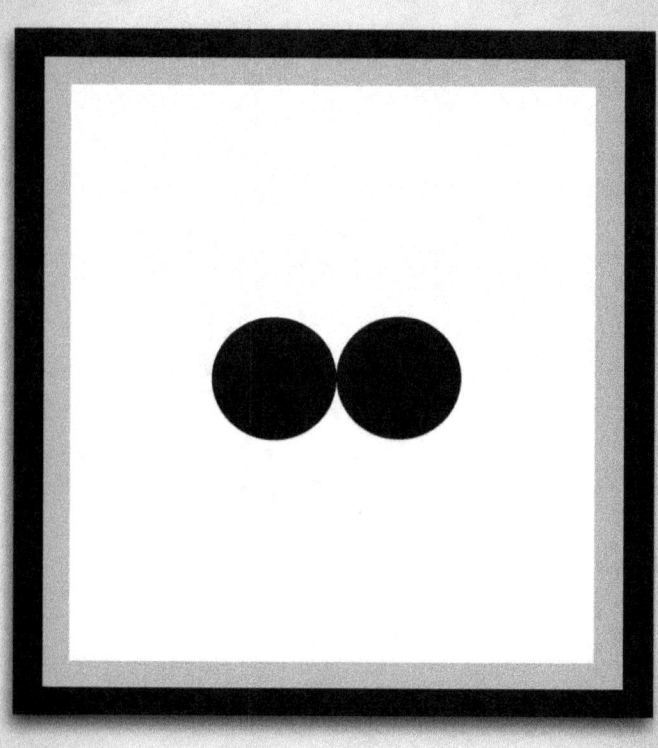

inappropriate

i got bored of this one
and quit sorry

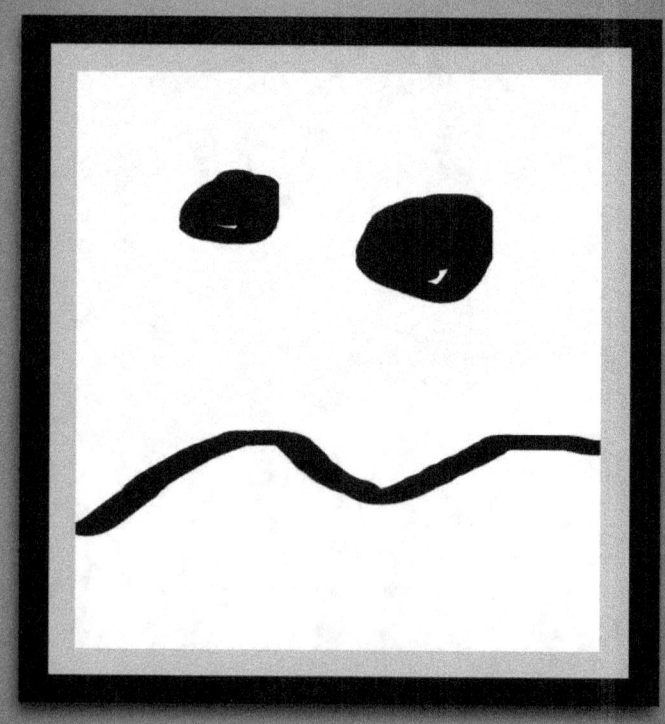

this is a little awkward

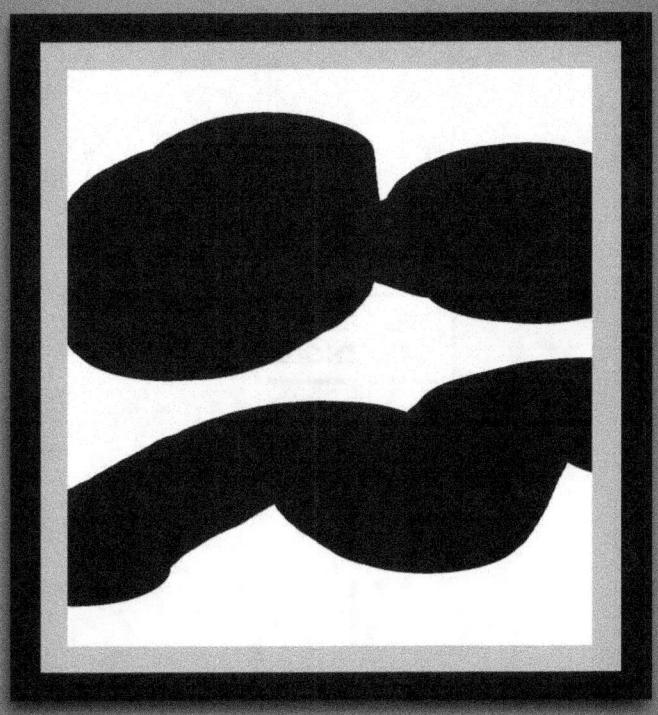

this is a big awkward

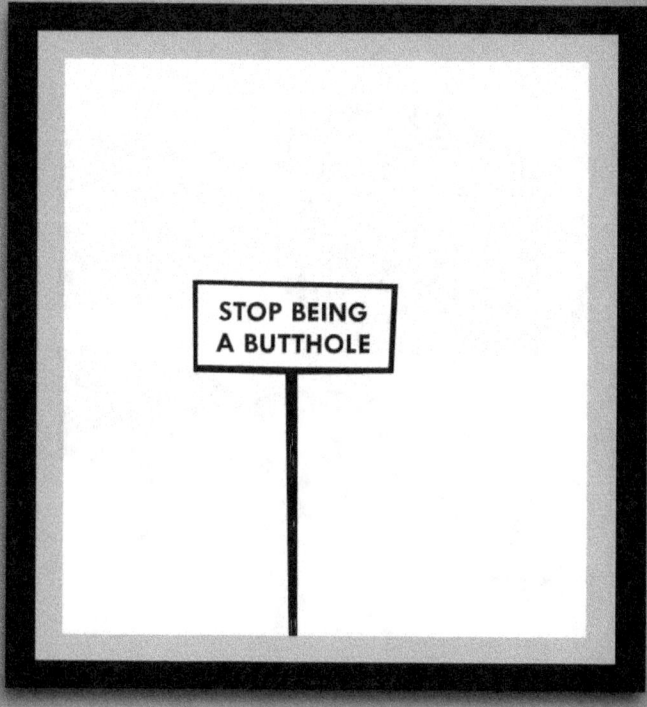

it's a sign from god

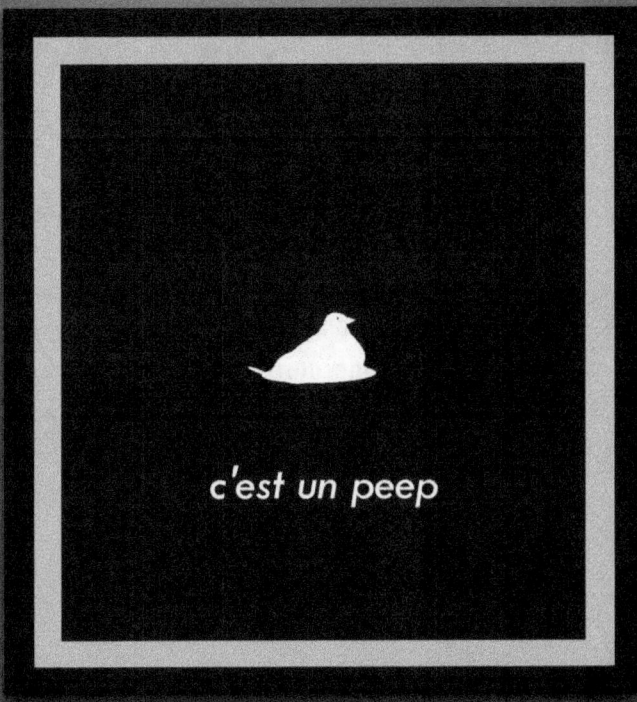

c'est un peep

you heard it here first folks

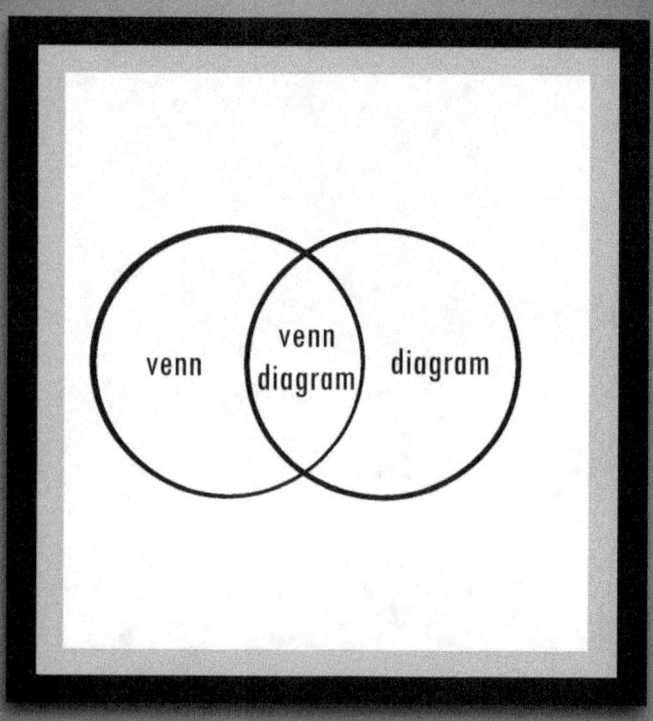

venn diagrams be like

stop reading

advice

whatever

well you rebel. just keep on going then abrasive twit

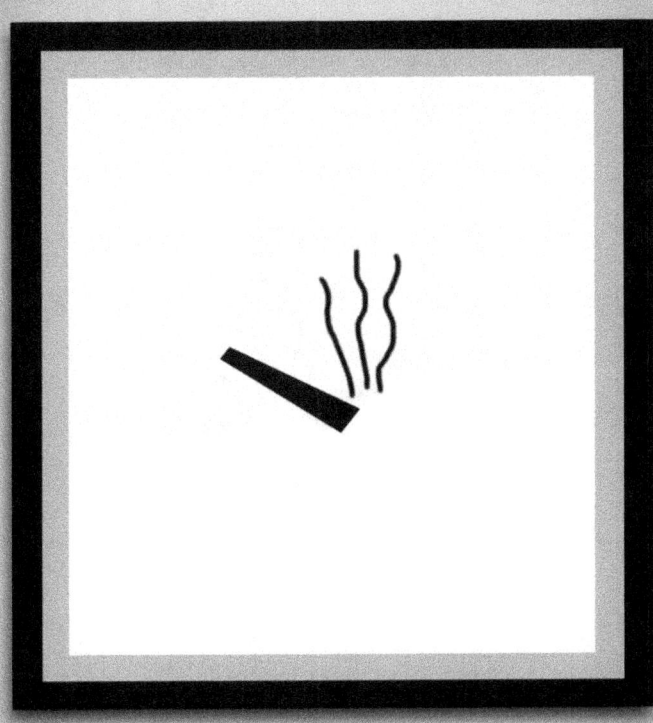

this are your drugs

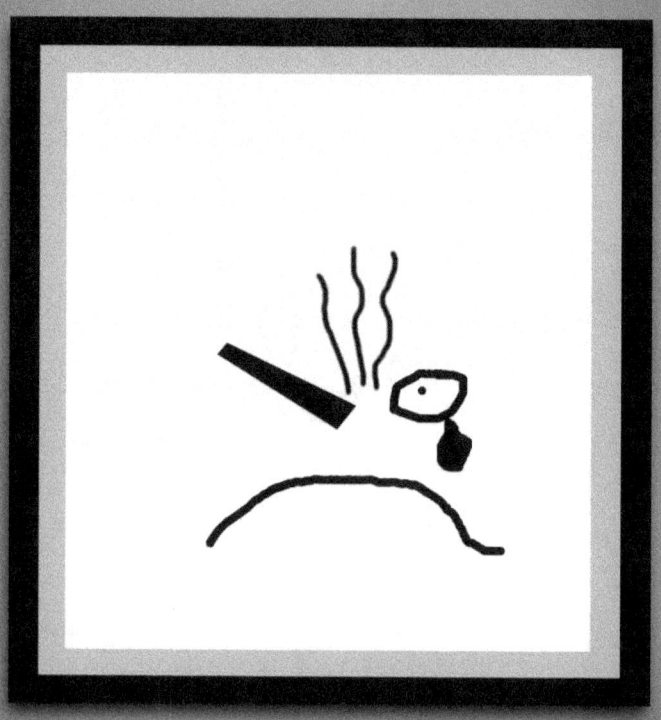

this are your drugs on
drugs

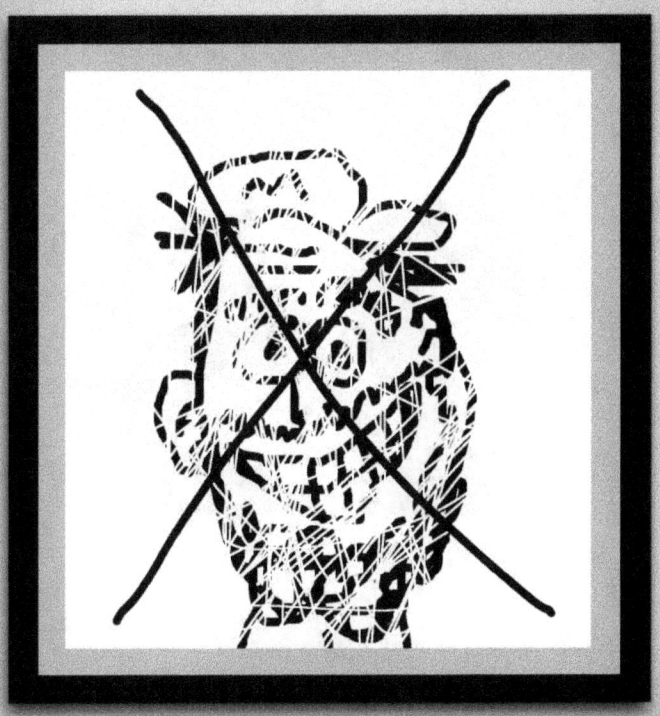

*nevermind i don't like
this one please don't
look at this oh god*

25

how many hours of
sleep i want to get a
night

self portrait but
zoomed out a lot

*self portrait but really
zoomed in a lot*

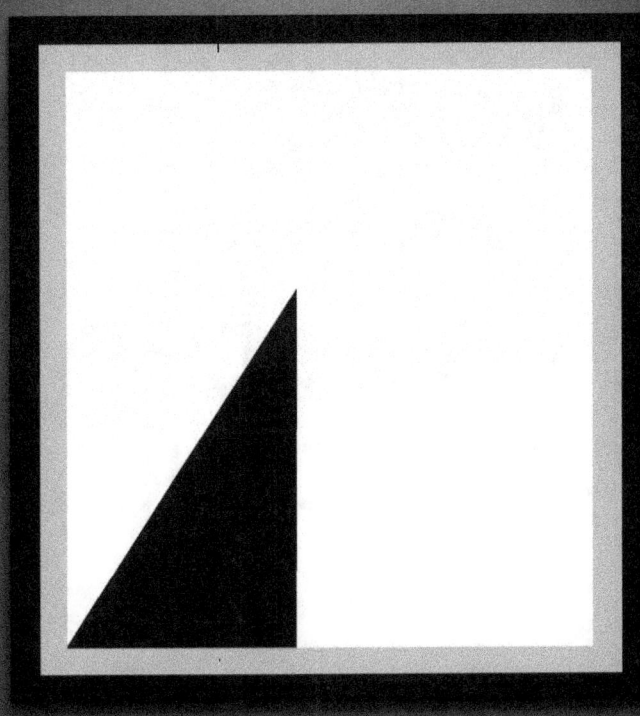

they say it's about the climb so here's a half-made mountain it's beautiful just the way it is

MUSIC CAN'T BE VISUALIZED YOU DORK

music visualized

i just left a smudge on
this canvas but hey that's
modern art for you mate

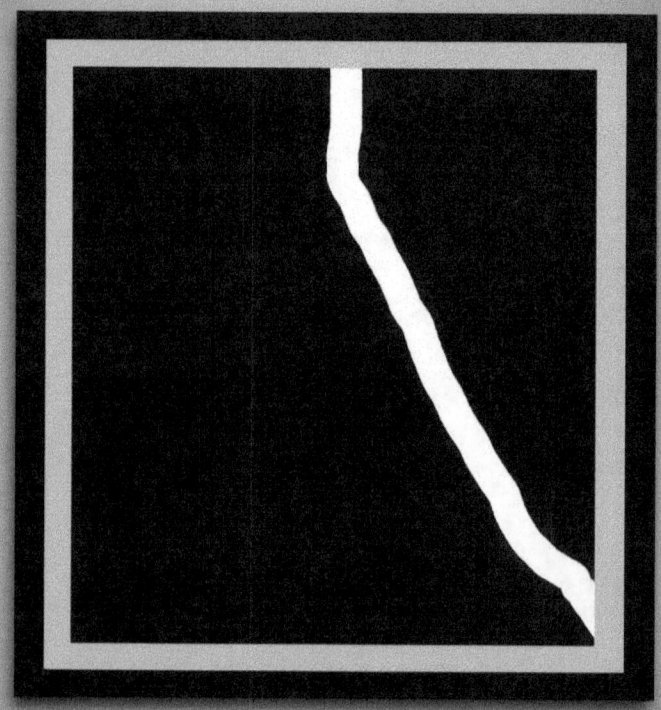

*mostly black but with a
little bit of white on it*

pick up lines to try

~~u r a funny typo on life~~

~~ur face would look good dead~~

~~i hate u but ironically~~

~~i actually just hate you~~

i apologize i accidently left my personal notes here

*this is a mirror, hey you
must be a vampire*

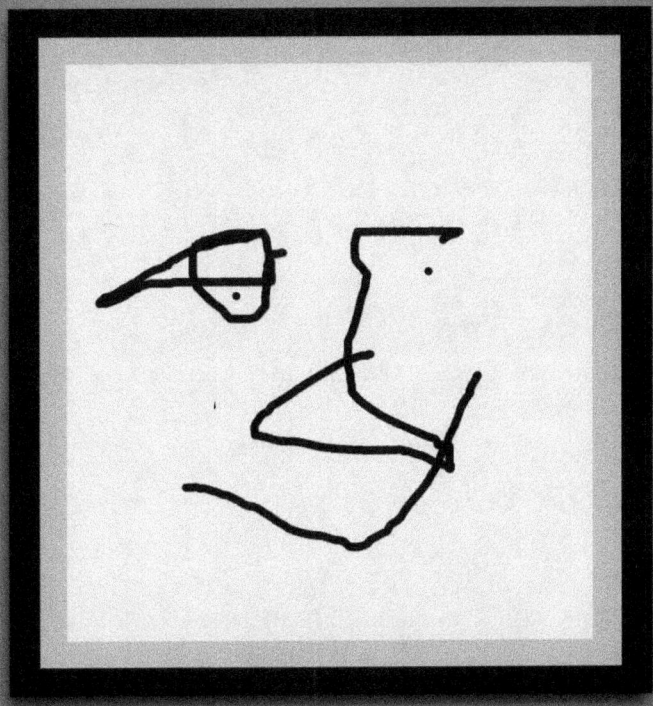

just kidding there's your reflection you ugly rascal

click x to close painting

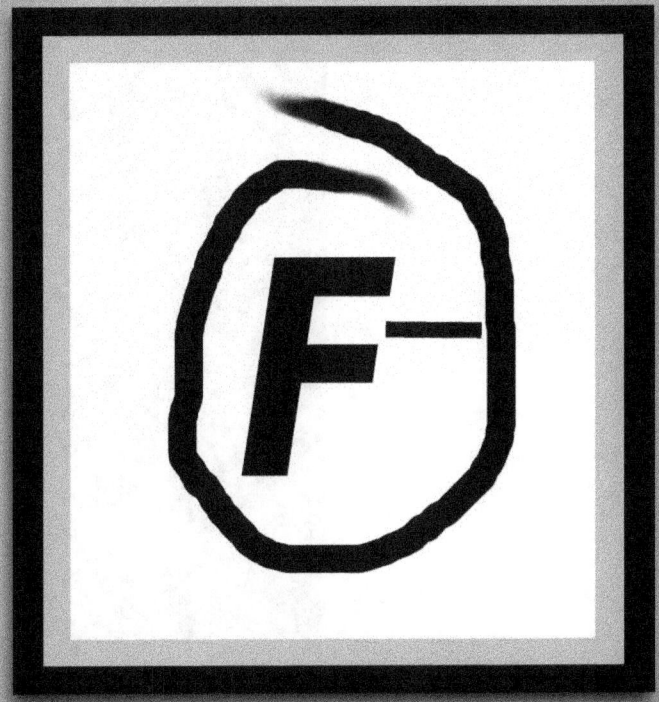

this painting failed its paint class

a white wall and a black
wall, would ya look how
great frens they are

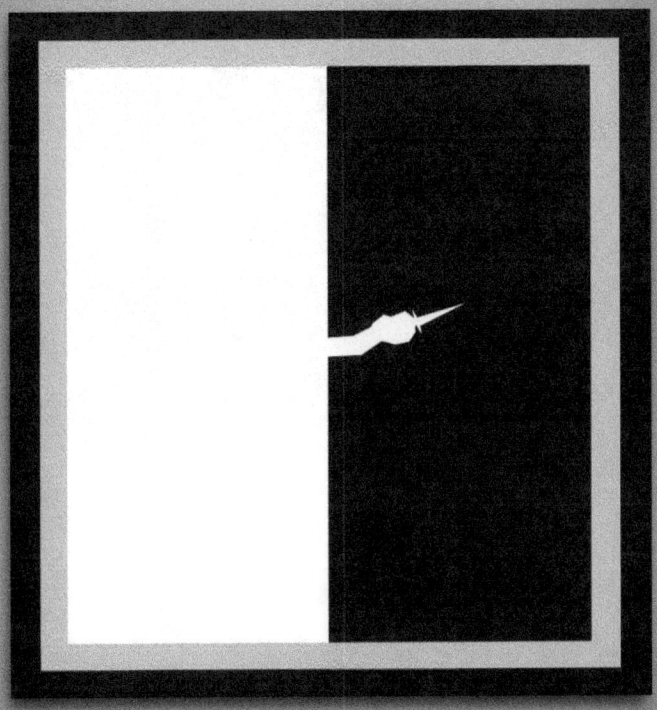

holy crap he stabbed
him quick turn the page
frick this

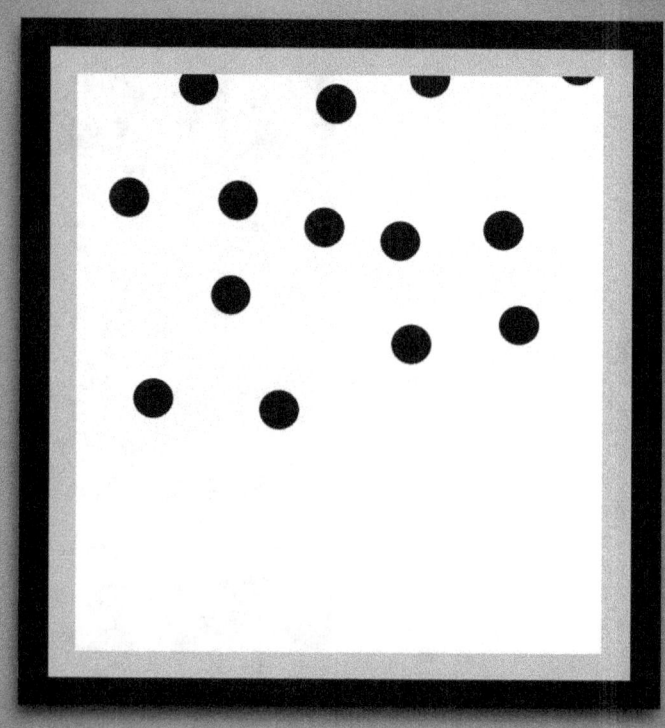

chocolate rain: when
black jesus cries

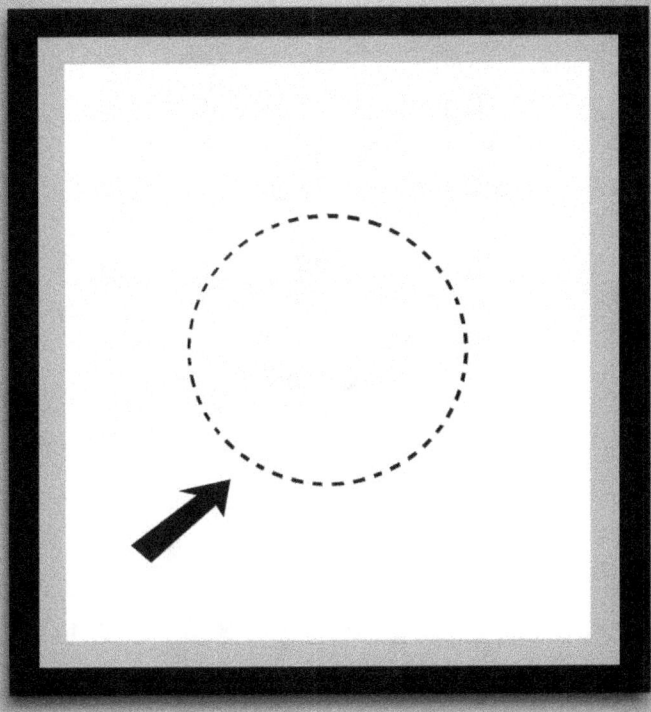

poke a hole through this with your finger

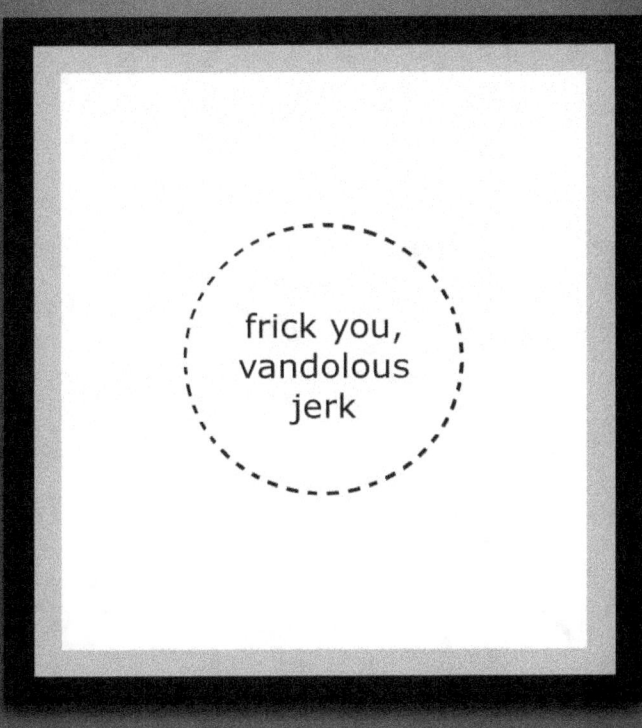

frick you,
vandolous
jerk

*this only exists for you to
see after you poked the
hole*

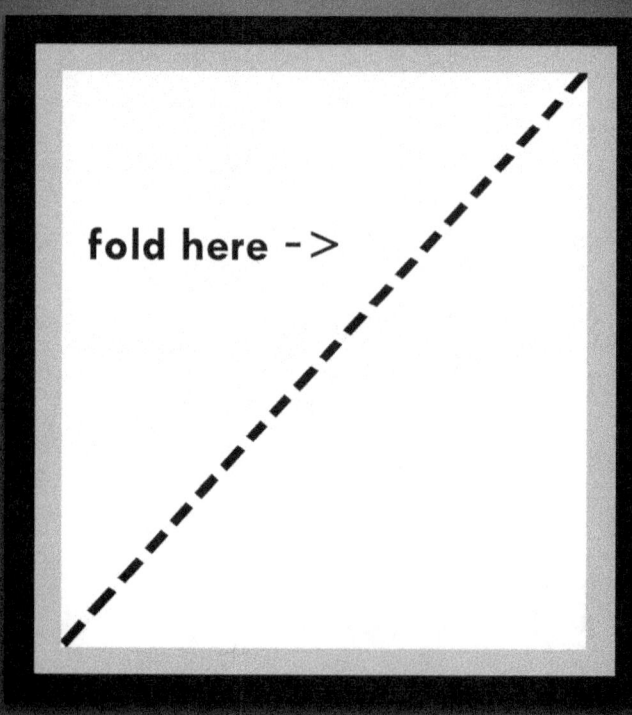

fold here ->

you hve made now a
successfully paper
airplane

SELF-DESTRUCT BUTTON

don't you freaking dare

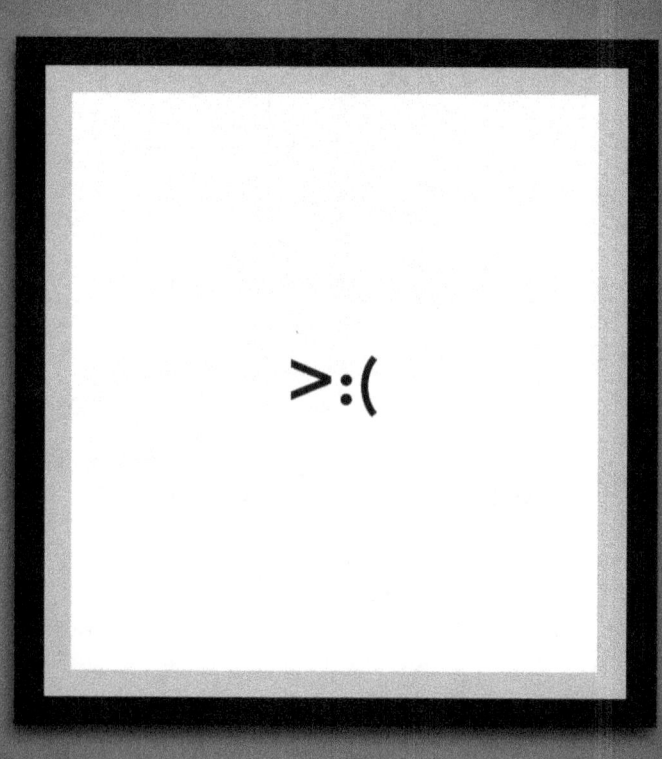

you button clicking rebel.
you're reason we keep the
real self-destruct button
on the back cover

i've run out of ideas to draw here so here's an elephant

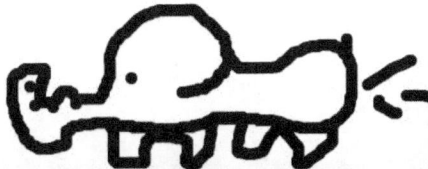

if you checked the back cover i'm going to freaking end you

i've got
a
ferrari

impressionism

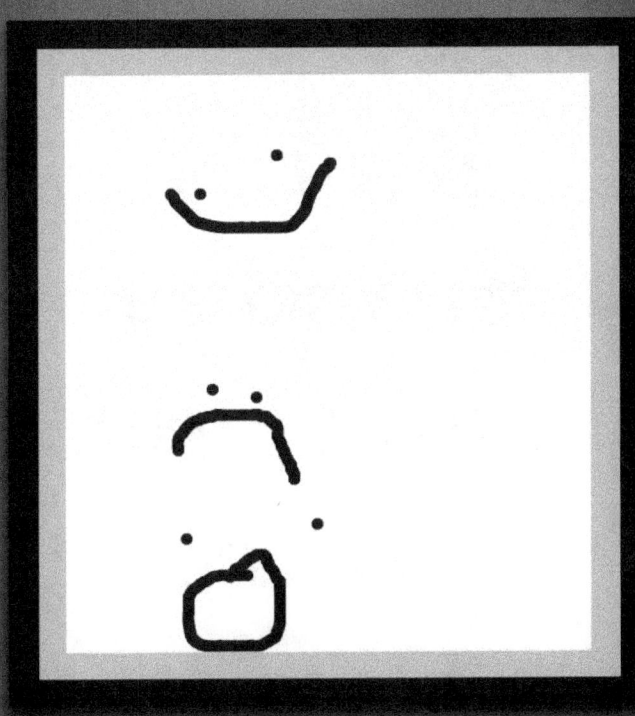

expressionism

it's my birthday what you get me

don't get anything he's a lying schmuck

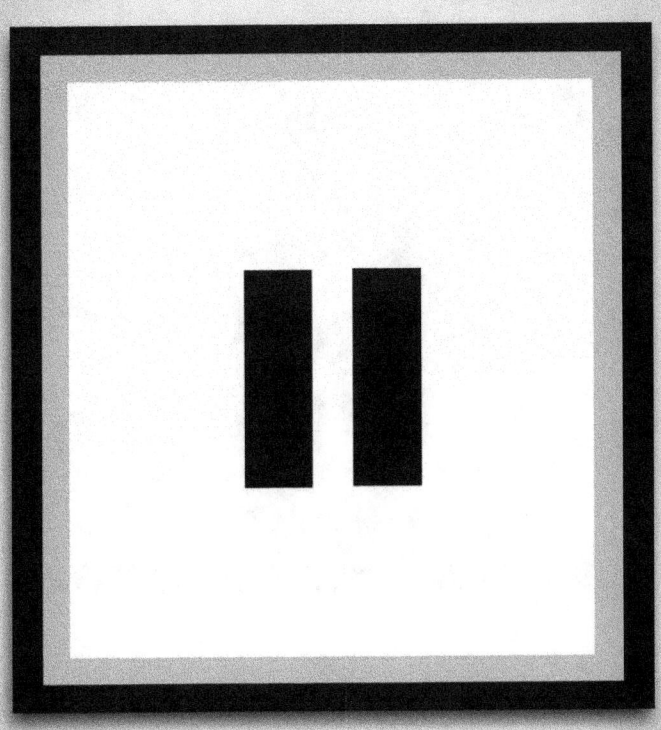

pause the book, go
outside and do something
active you fat frick

o frick this one fell

**help me
up please**

where is the lamp on this
painting, the frick

*this was inspired by a
good friend of mine
Stevie Wonder*

my good friend Stephen
Hawking helped me
draw this one

tribute to the life and
work of a good friend of
mine michael jackson

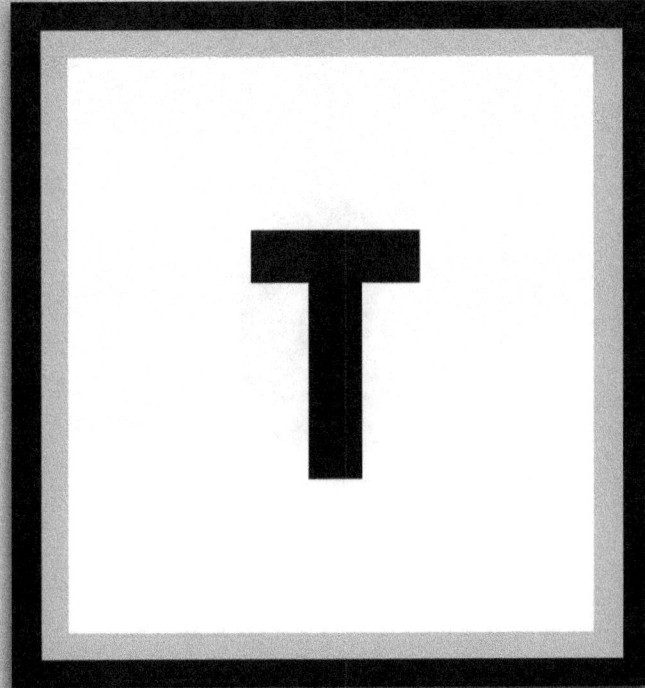

mr. t

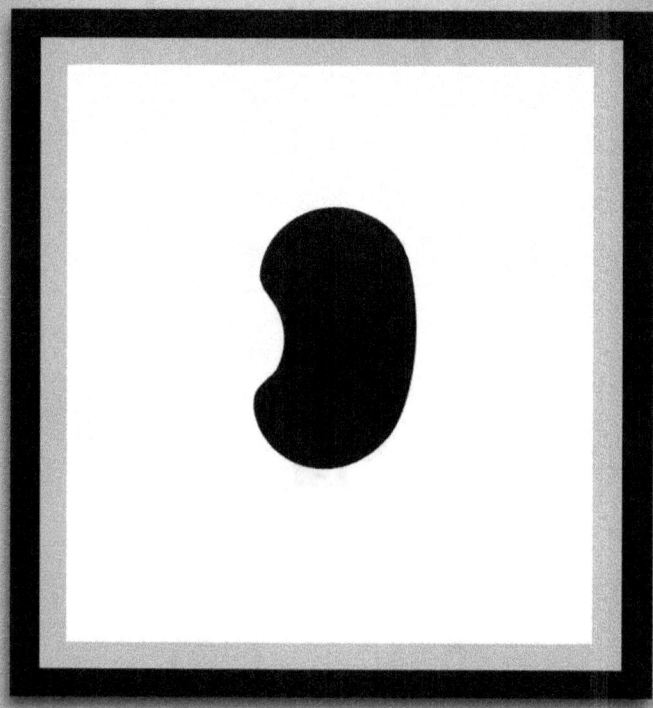

mr. bean

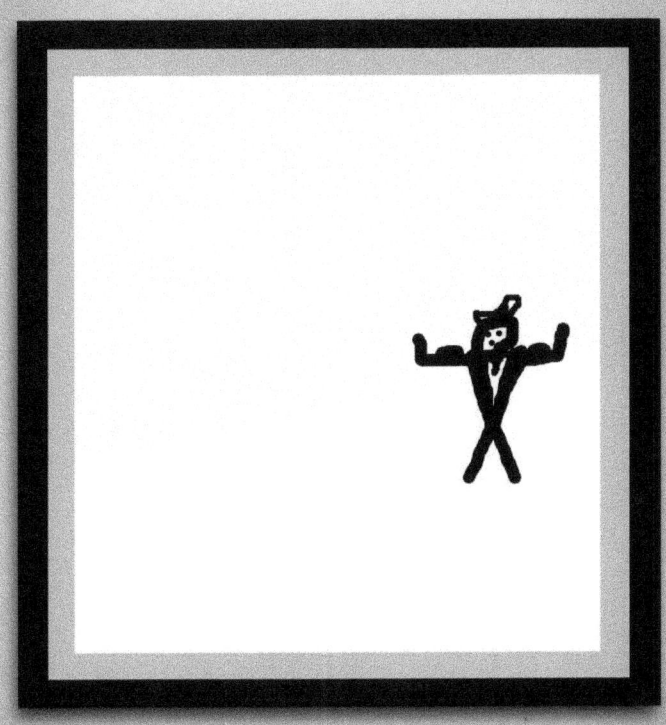

mr. right

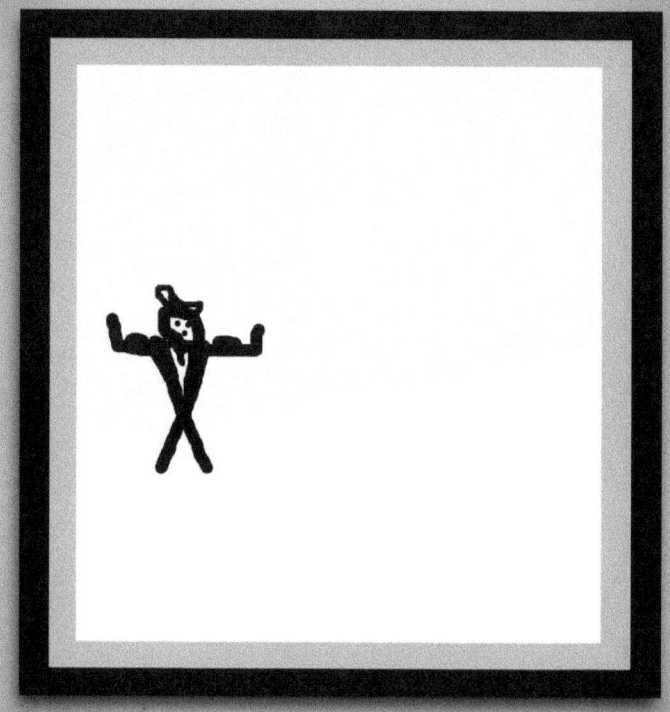

mr. left

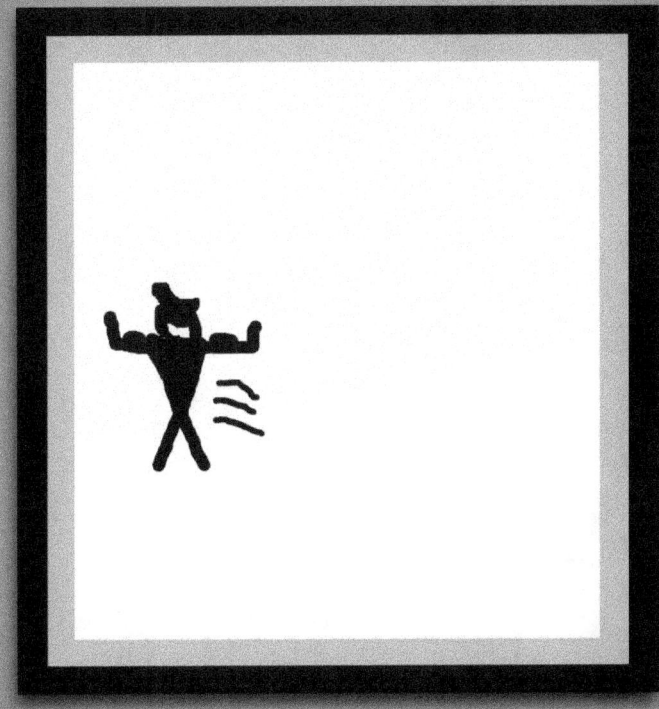

mr. leaving

mr. hyde

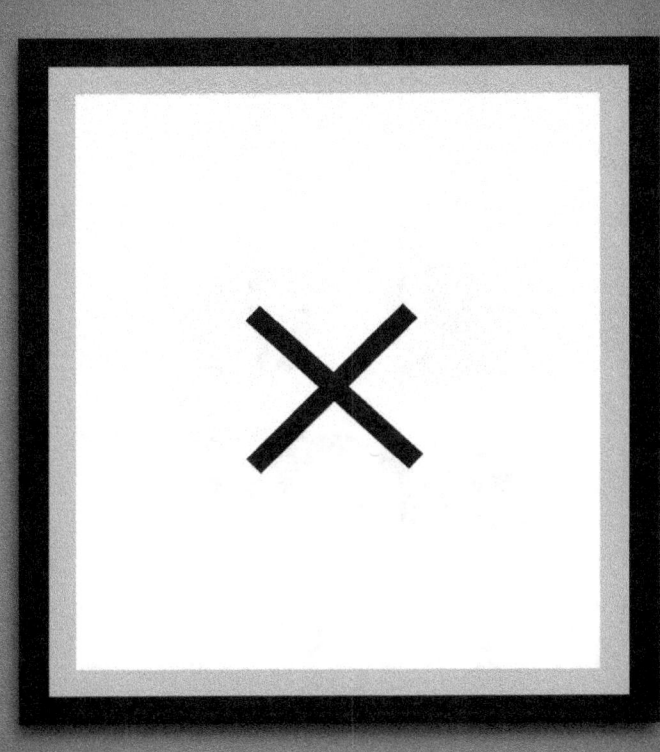

lick the x

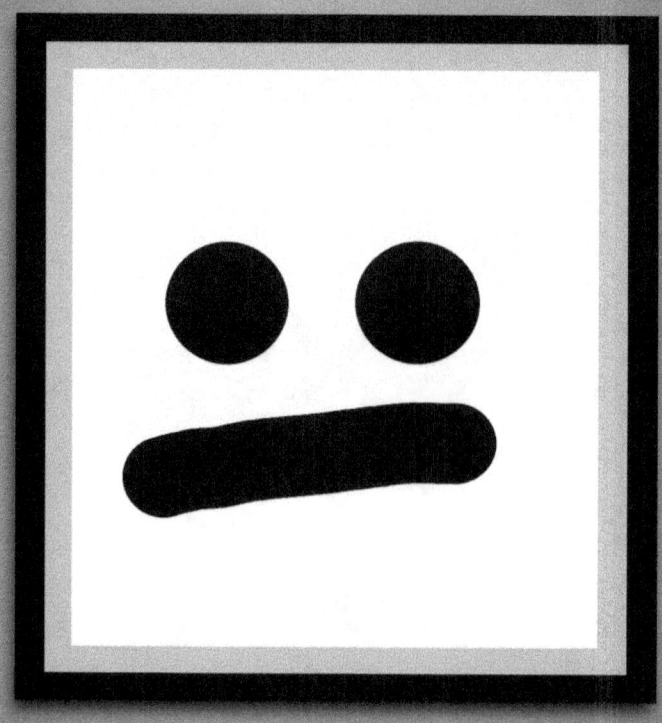

you're disgusting, go see
a counselor

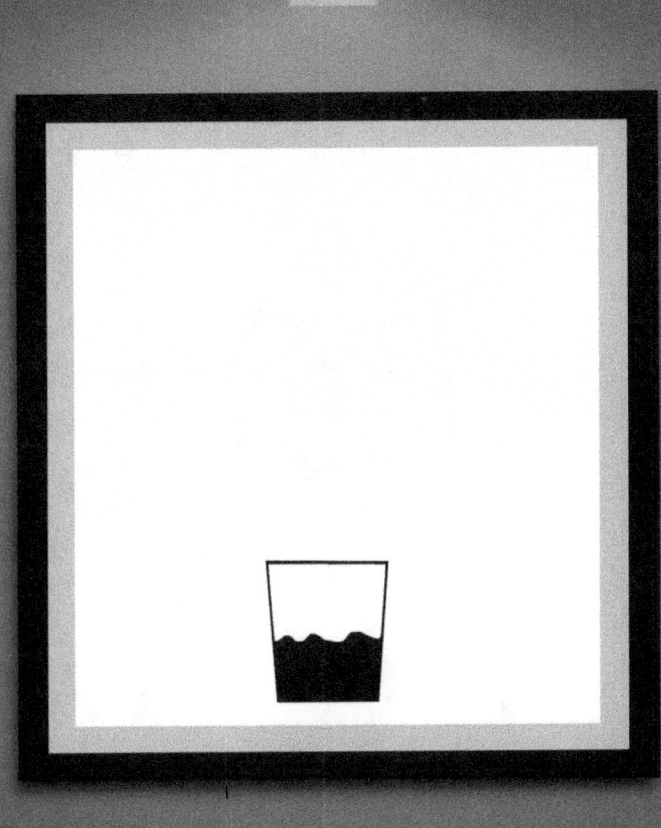

attractive cup of water

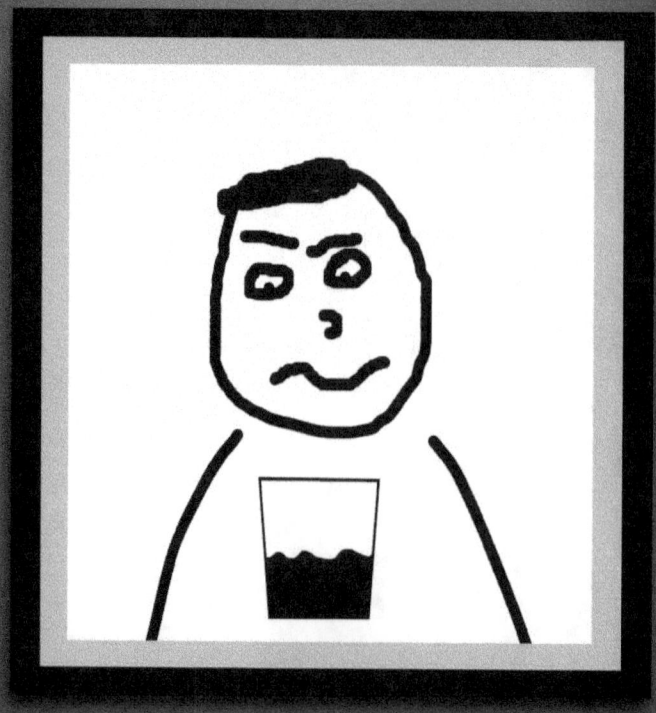

reader trying to figure
out why the water is
black

RACIST

what the heck why do you care what color the water is you freaking biggot

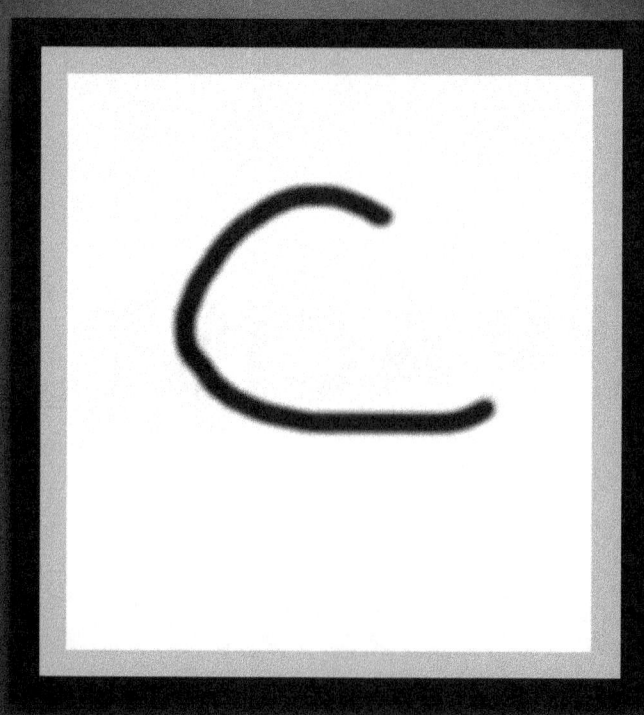

did you c what i did there

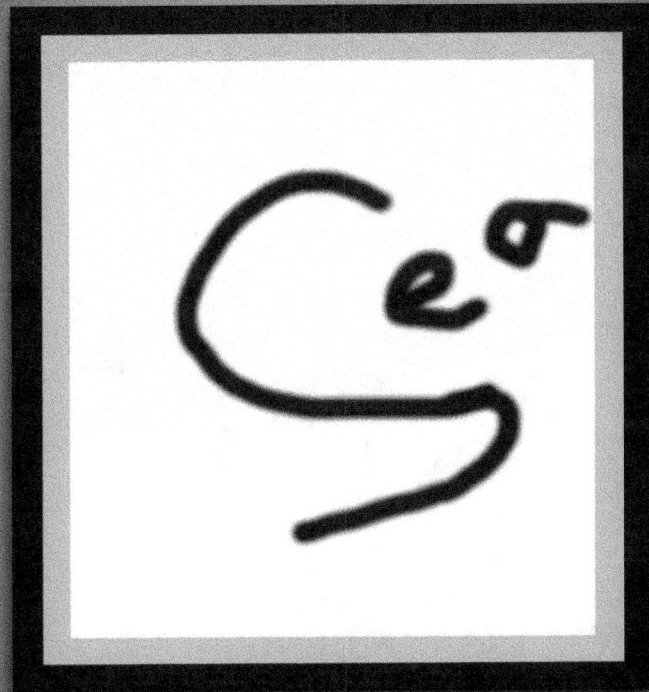

did you sea what i did there

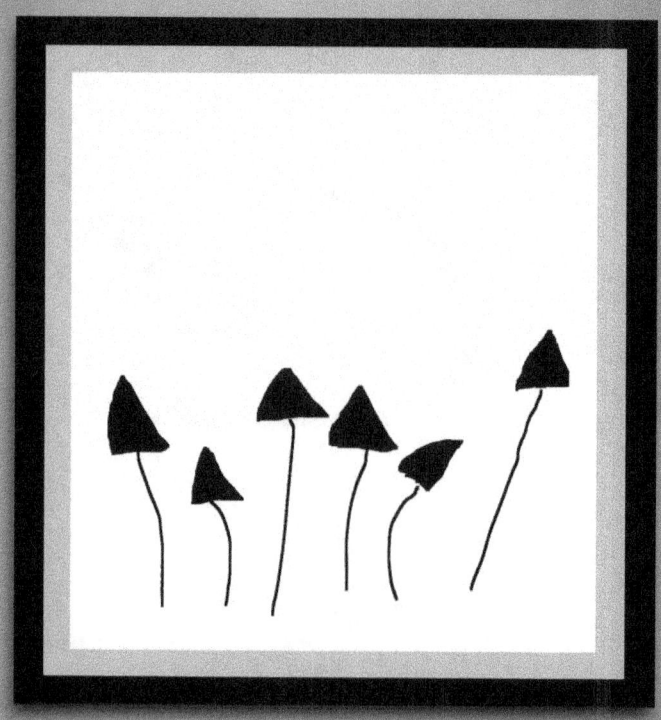

look here i've made some
funny looking trees

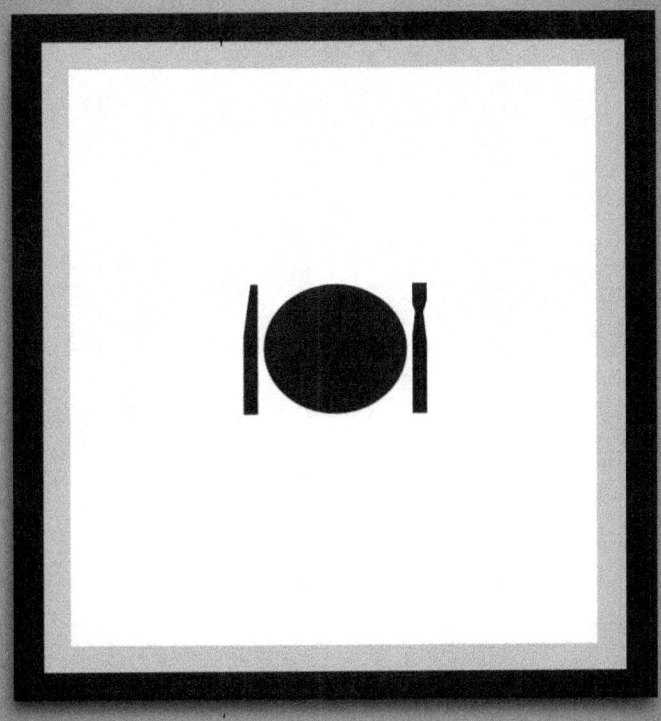

look here i've made some
funny looking trees

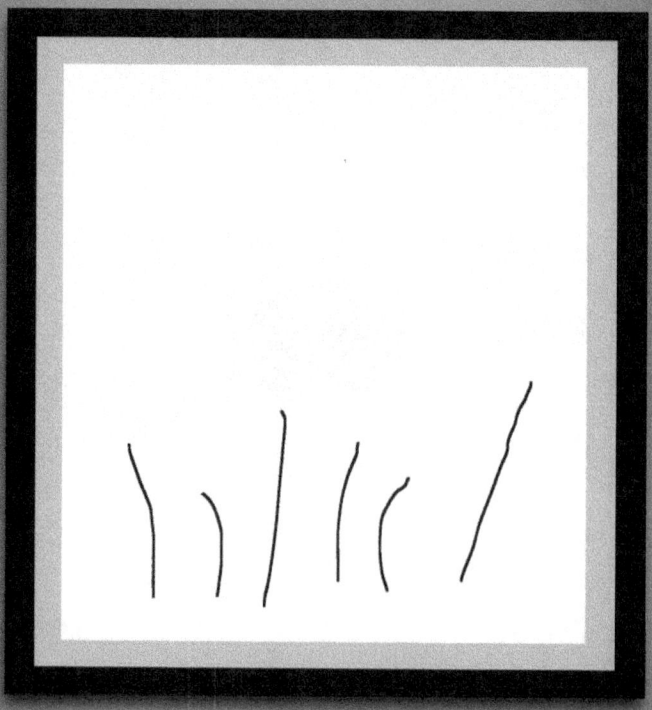

haha, i have fooled you,
those were mushrooms,
silly rabbit

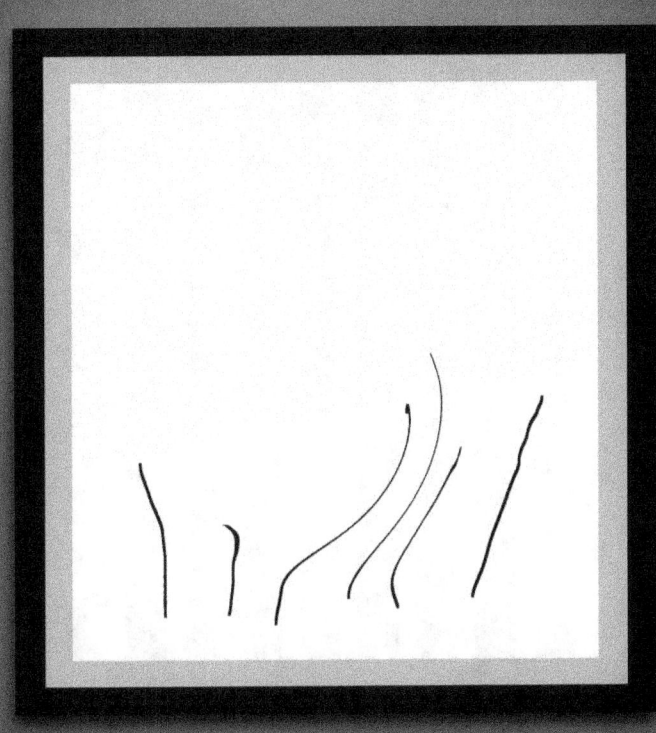

now your brain is all
funky, you bad bad boi

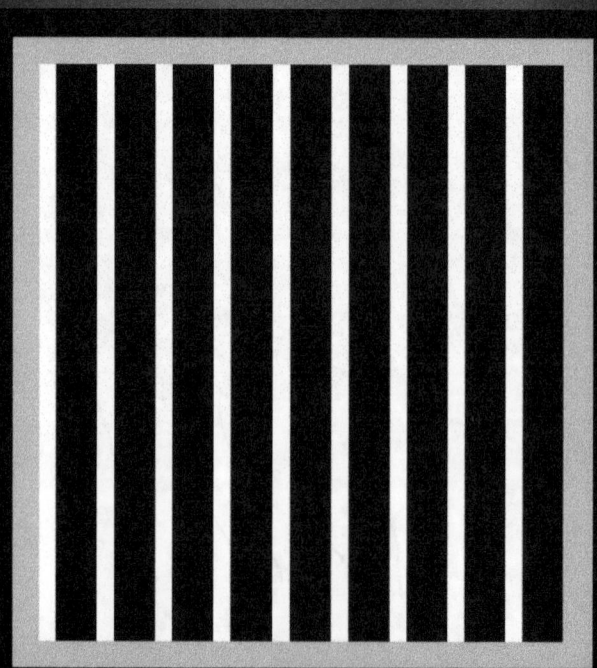

bro you got caught my dude now the government is paying to feed you as a punishment.

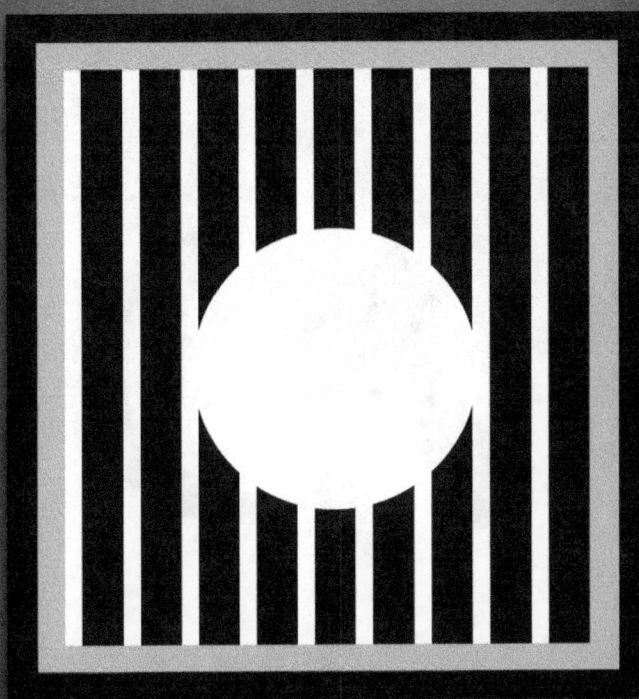

you have escaped, all you had to do was to paint a circle

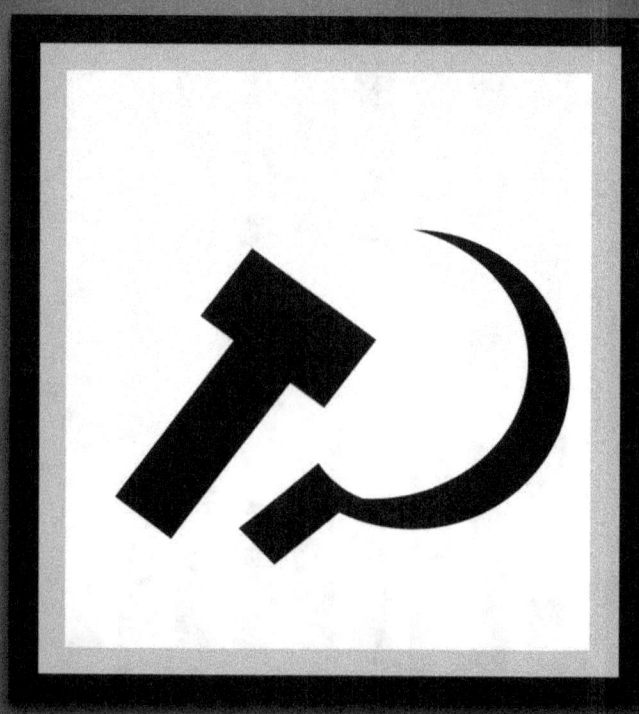

now that you've escaped prison seize the means of production, take that trump!

Loading...

gotta wait for this one

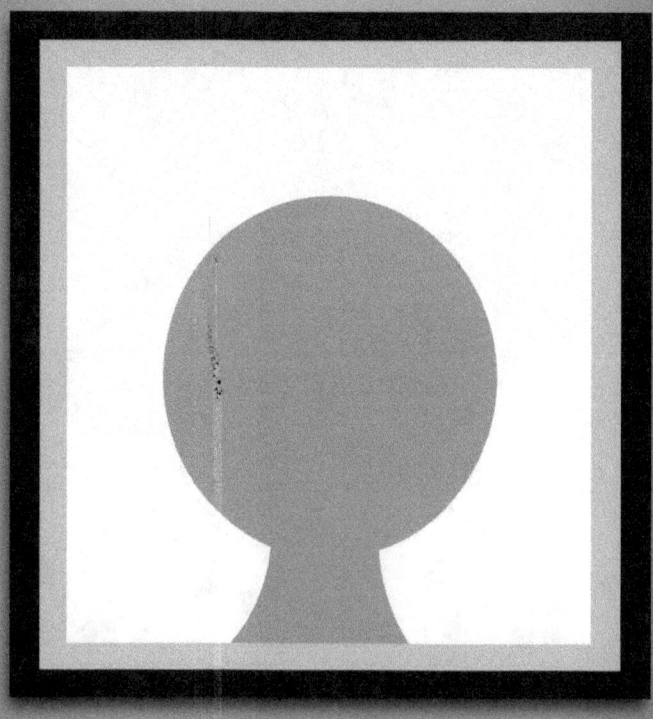

*hey move you're blocking
the painting*

o snap
    you have become

meta'd

welcome to utter
    transcendence

u r not in a art gallery

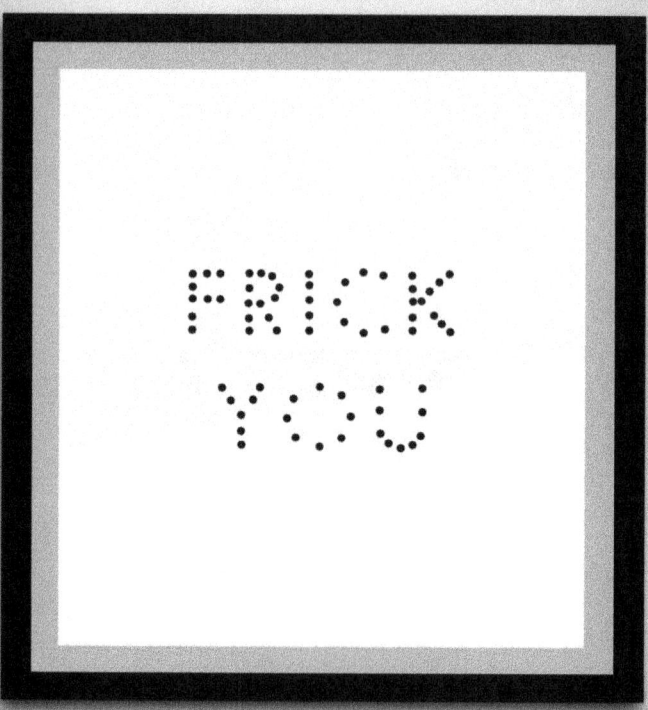

this is one of those fun
connect the dots try it heh

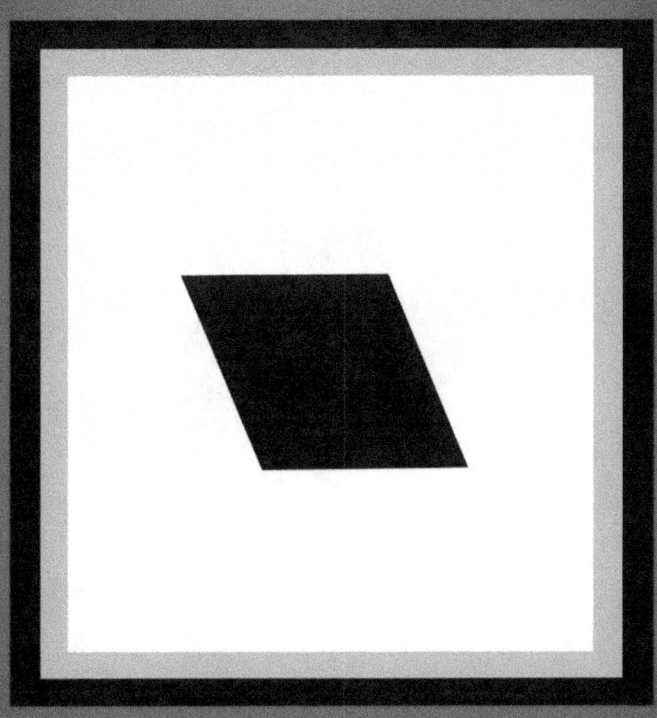

see this trapezoid?
remember it well... don't
you forget it

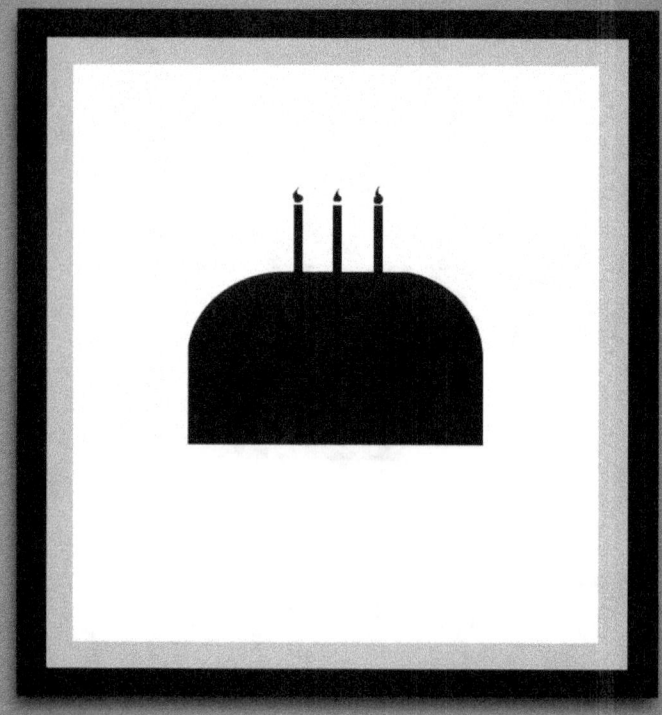

my favorite food

JK cake's a lie my
favorite's pie, your life's
is a lie, go die in a hole

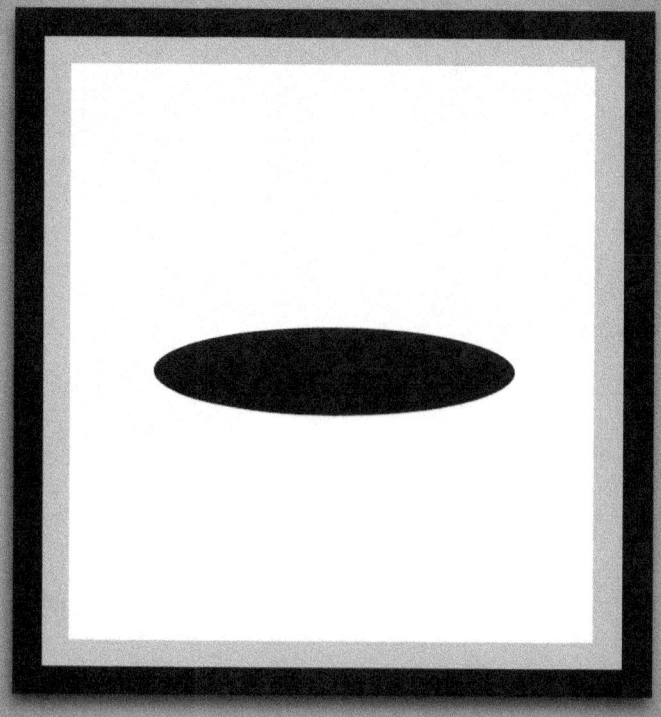

here's the hole

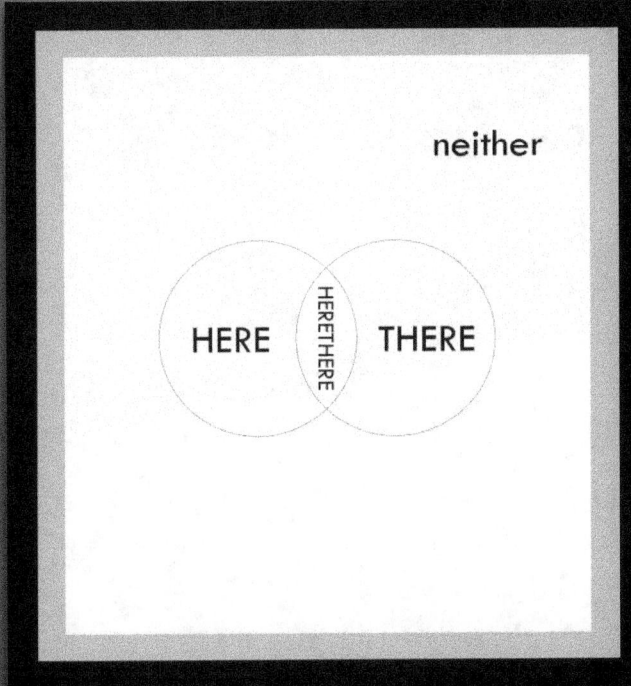

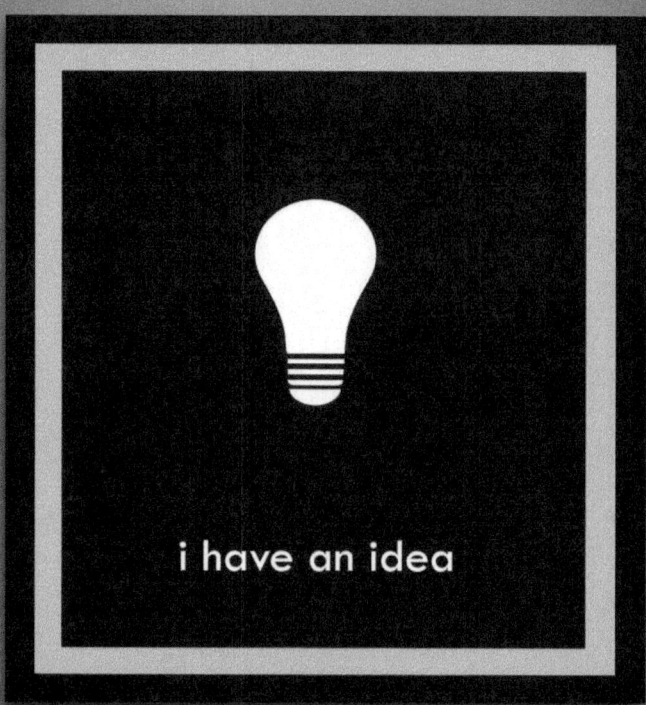

i have an idea

my idea was drawing a
lightbulb

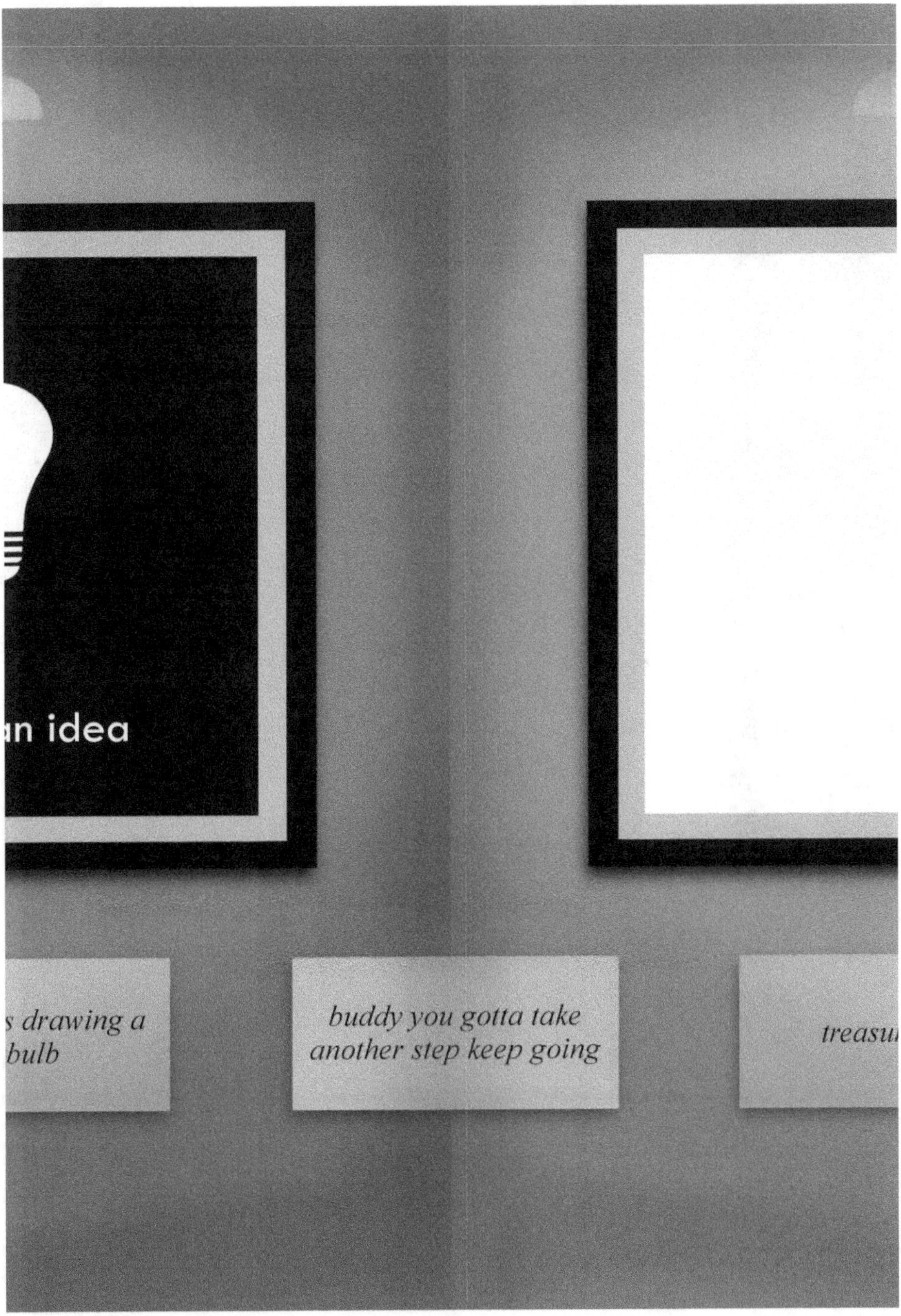

an idea

s drawing a
bulb

*buddy you gotta take
another step keep going*

treasu

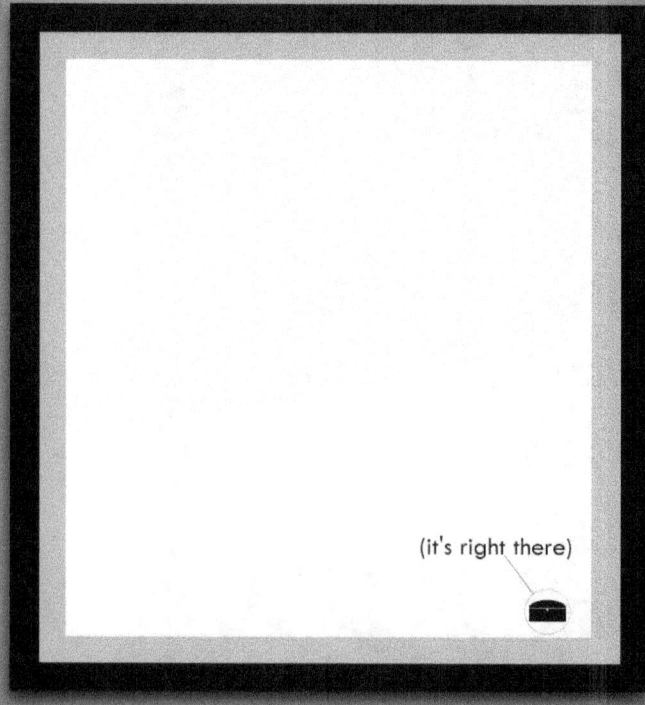

(it's right there)

treasure hunt

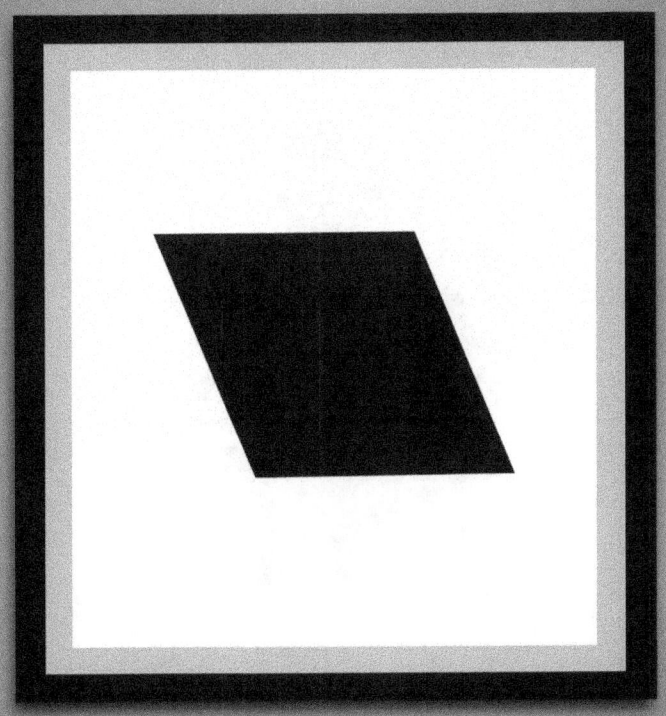

THERE IT IS AGAIN,
THE TRAPEZOID BACK
WITH A HEARTY
VENGEANCE

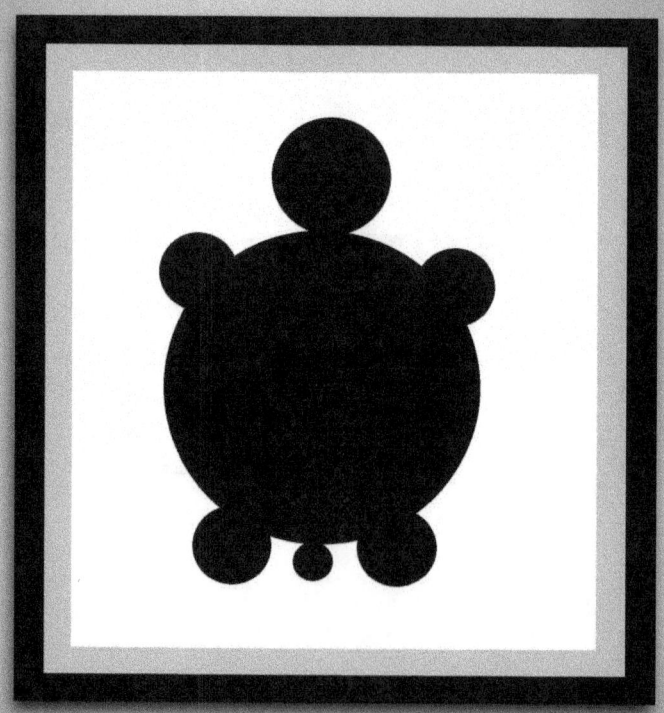

this mr. turtl, turtles are
super slow

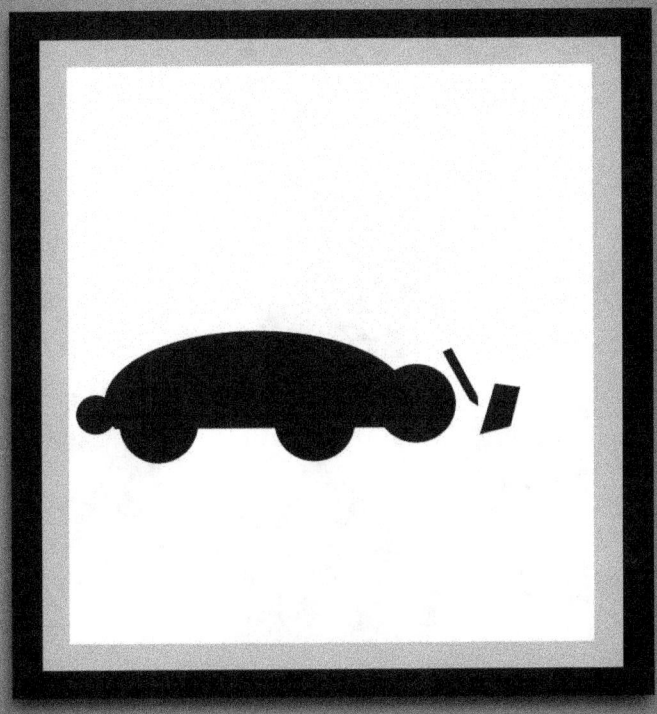

*mr. turtl is especially
slow, he tests poorly*

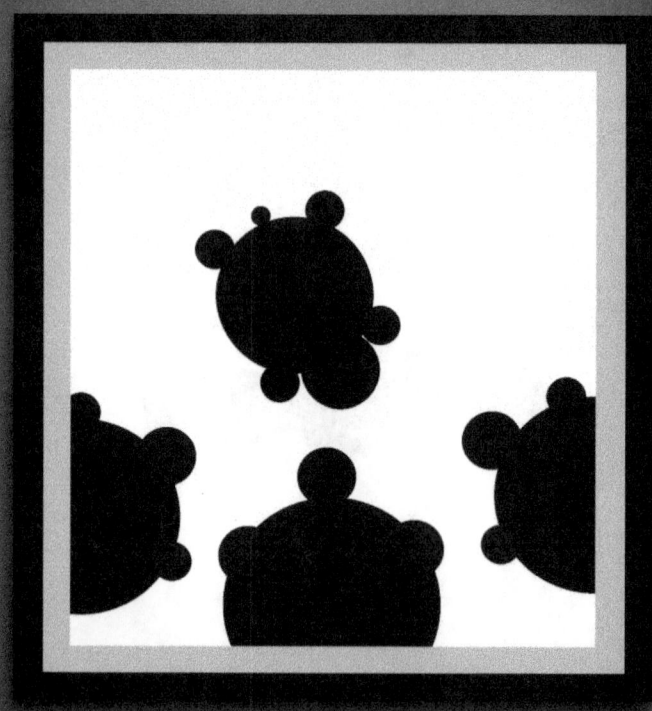

the other turtle children
made fun of mr. turtle

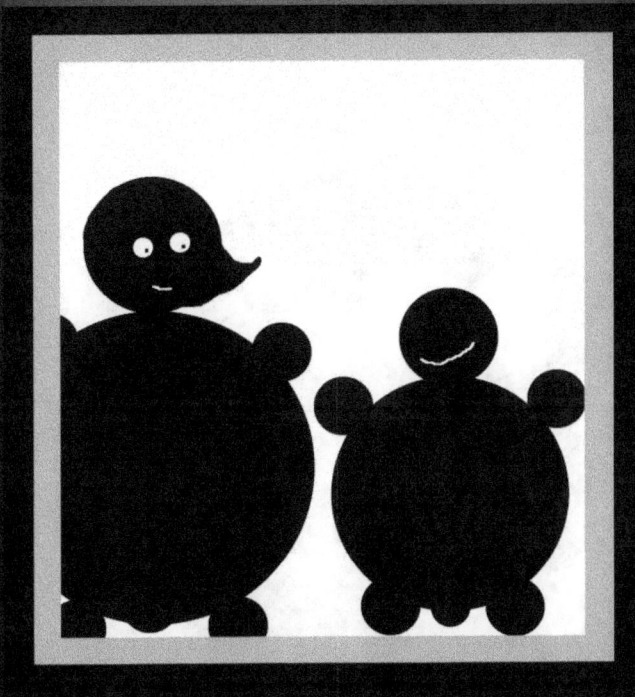

when he goes home his
mommy tells him he is
loved, and all the pain
melts into the background

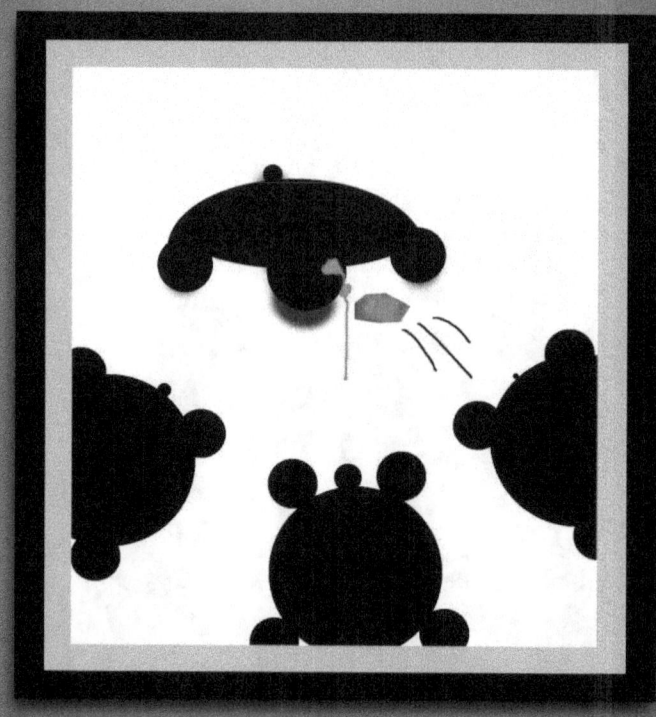

one day the children start
to throw rocks at mr.
turtl's face. mommy's
words don't help that

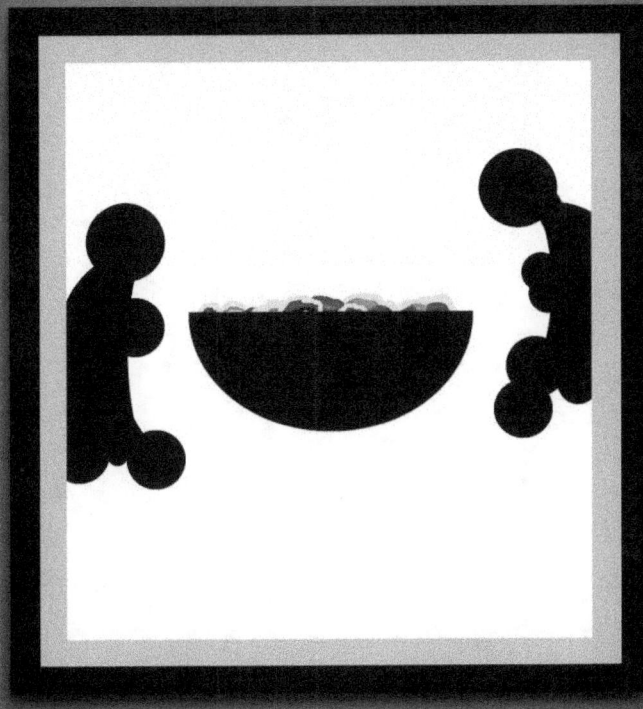

mr. turtl is now slow turtl soup, now are you glad you laughed at him? dweeb.

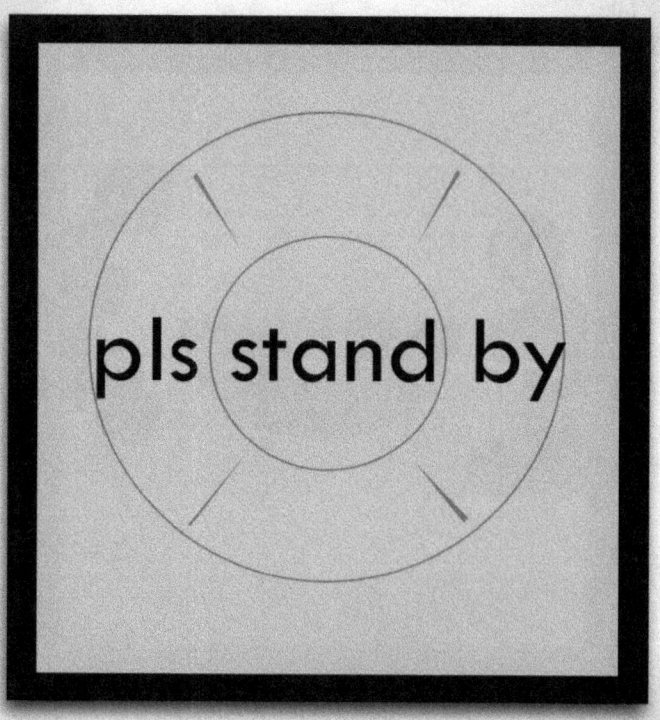

pls stand by

time for a wee wee break.
join me as we readers all
collectively micturate
i'll race u

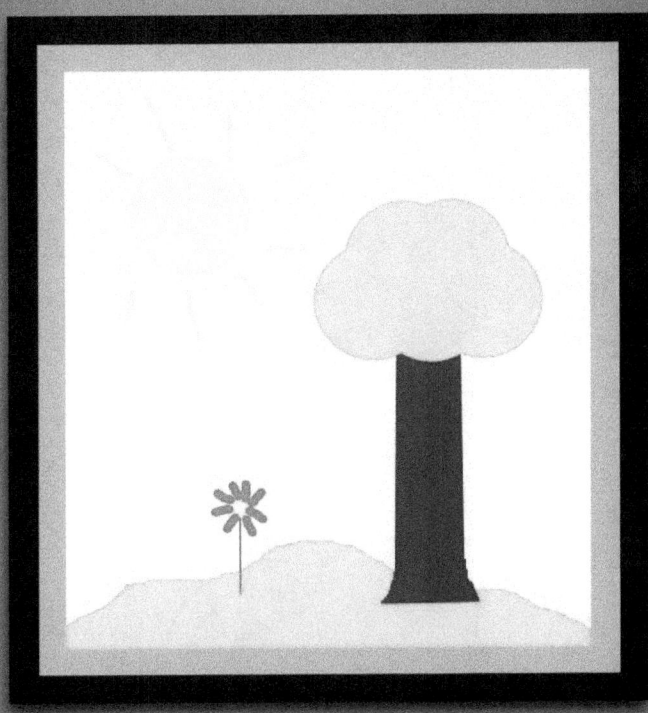

you drew this as a kid
too right?

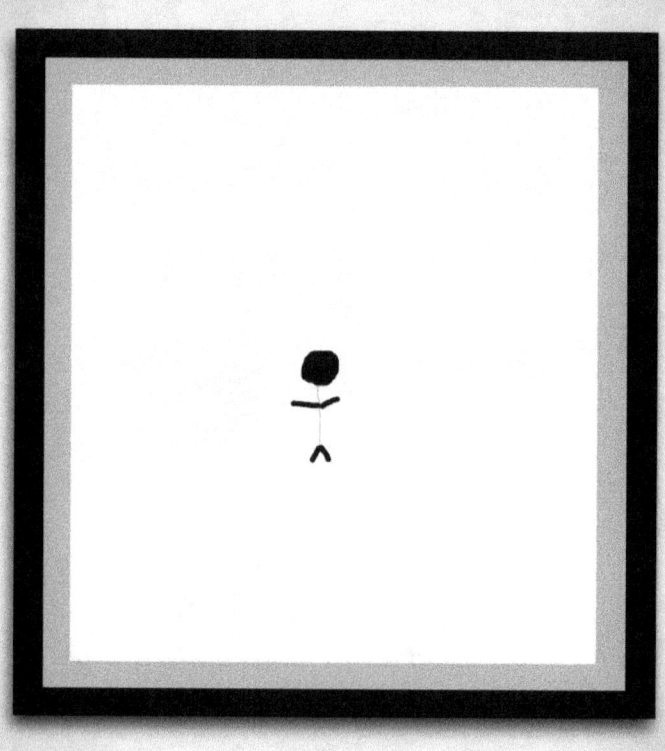

slender maen

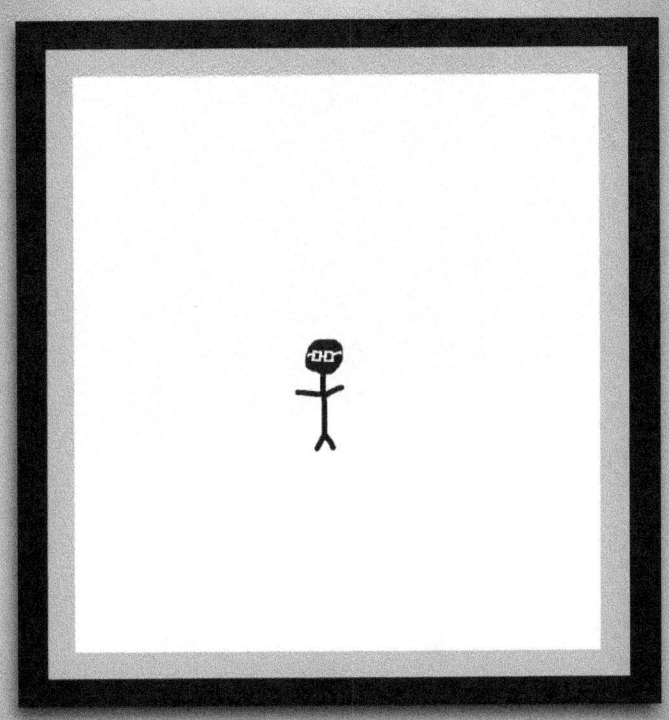

lol this frickin' nerd

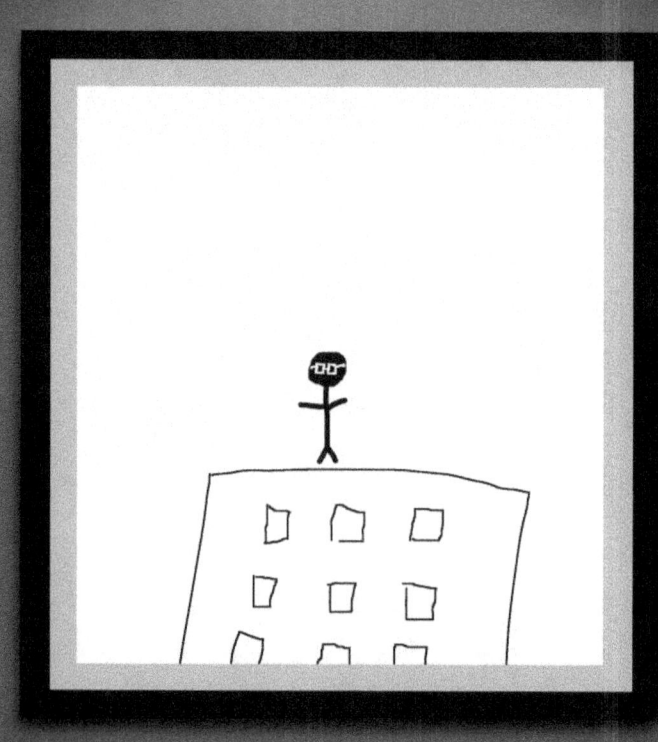

oh frick now he owns microsoft that sure betrayed my expectations what good art that is right there wow

THIS BOOK DOESN'T GET ANY FUNNIER SORRY

apology

Poop

lol wall art

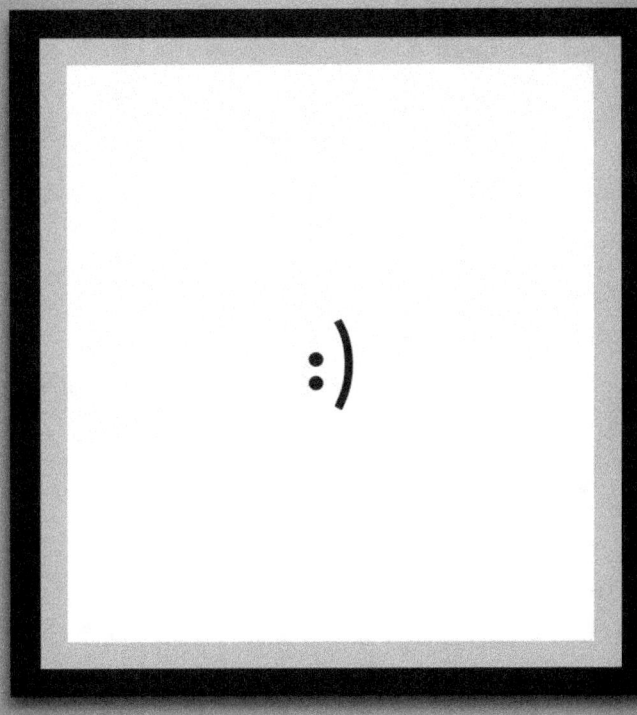

smilie

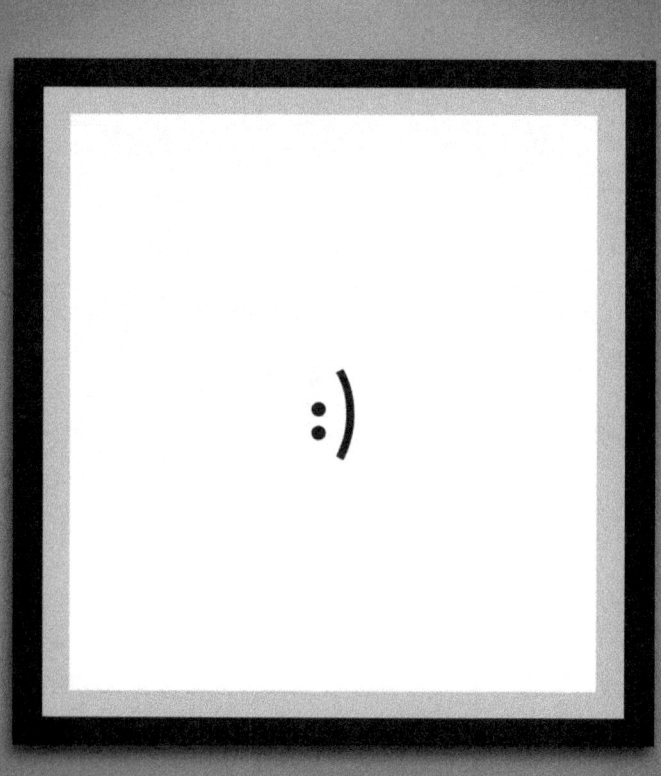

smilie after being called
beautiful

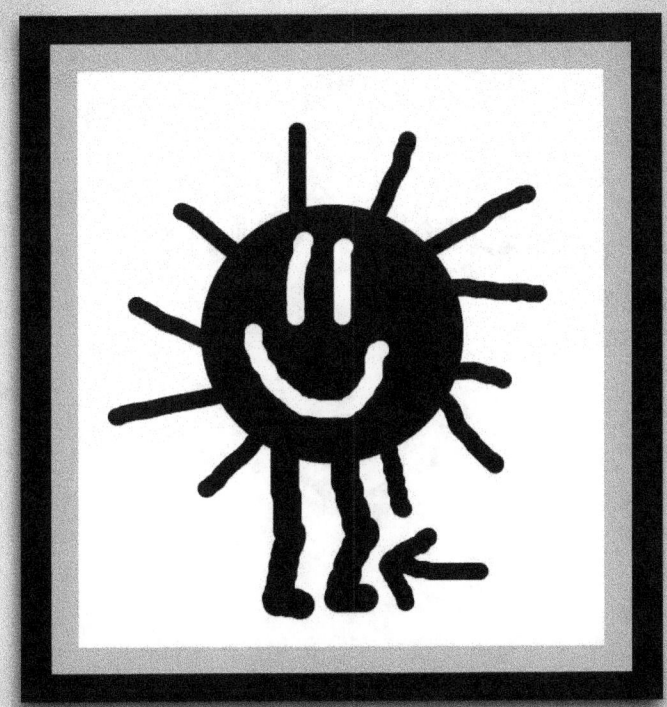

sunshin

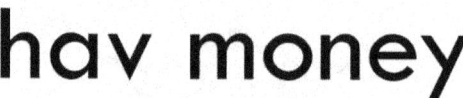

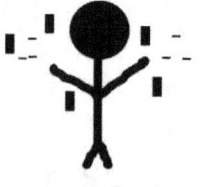

how to be a successful

i'm like so sorry my
printer broke on this one
excuse me

really bad

skunk smell visualized

INTRO TO FREAKIN' ACCOUNTING 101

literally hell

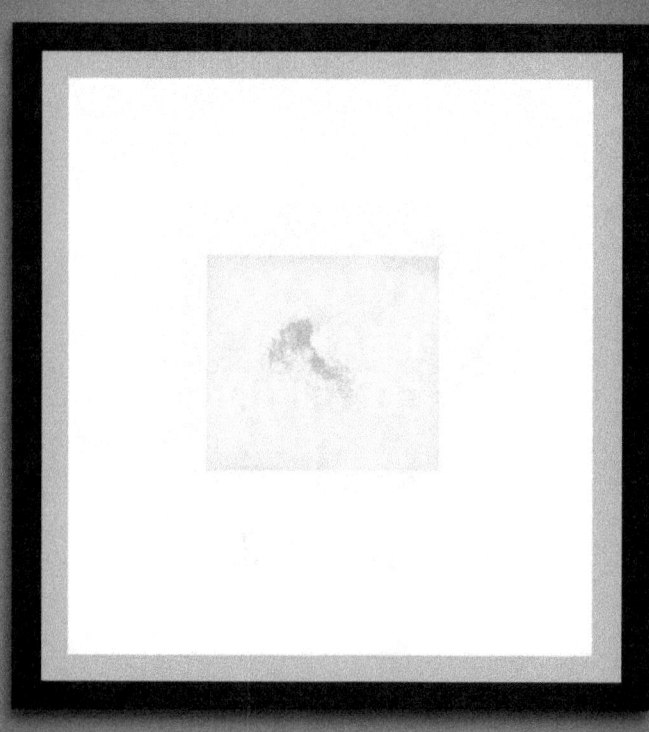

used napkin

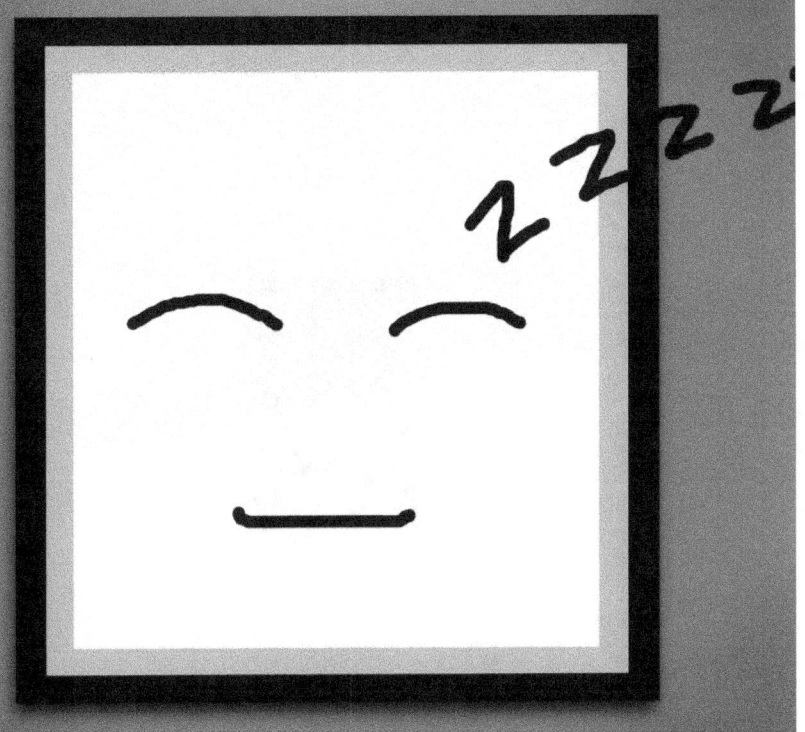

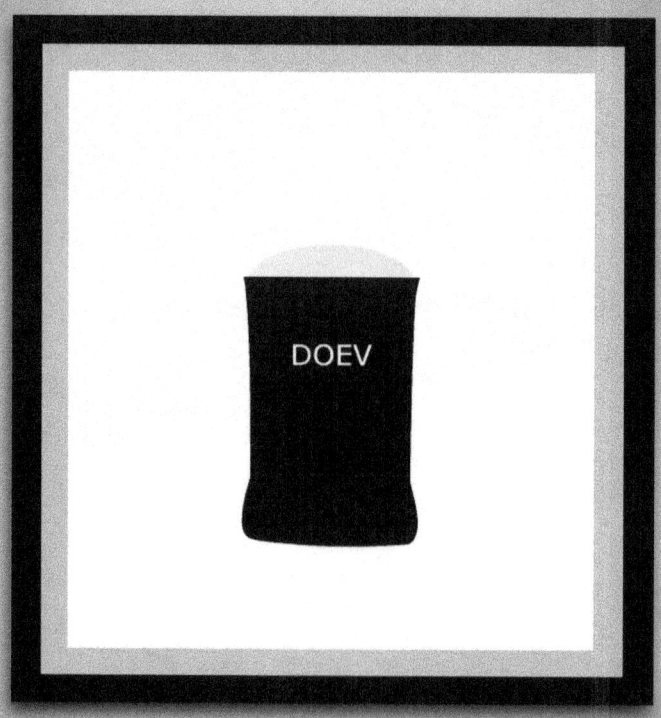

oh there, i've been looking
for this for a month!

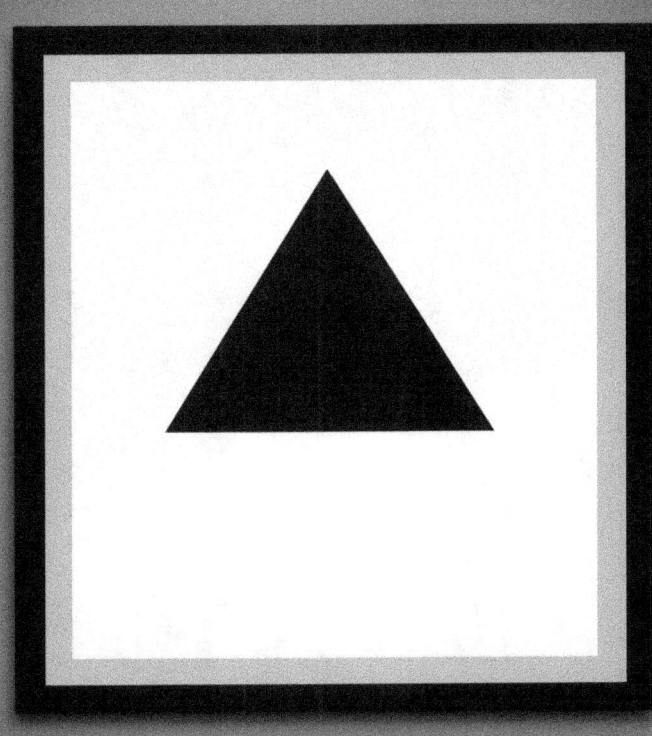

dis art is illuminate

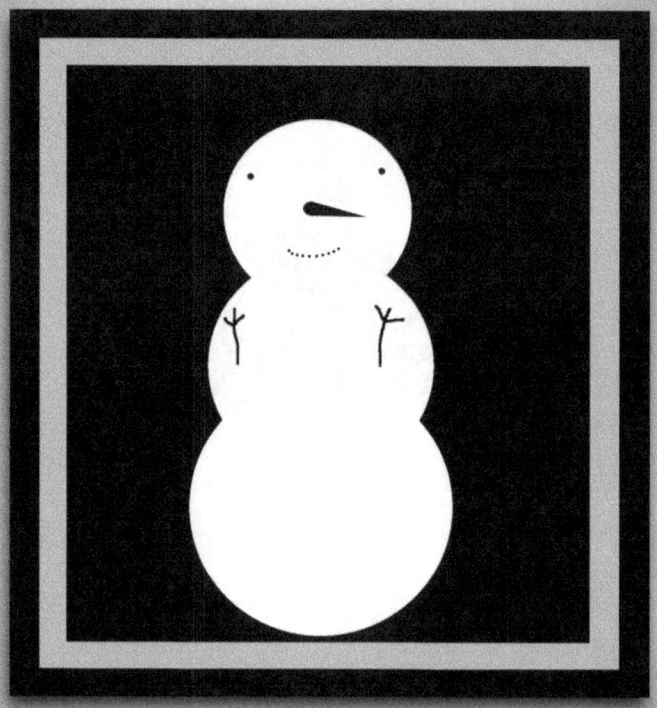

robert frost

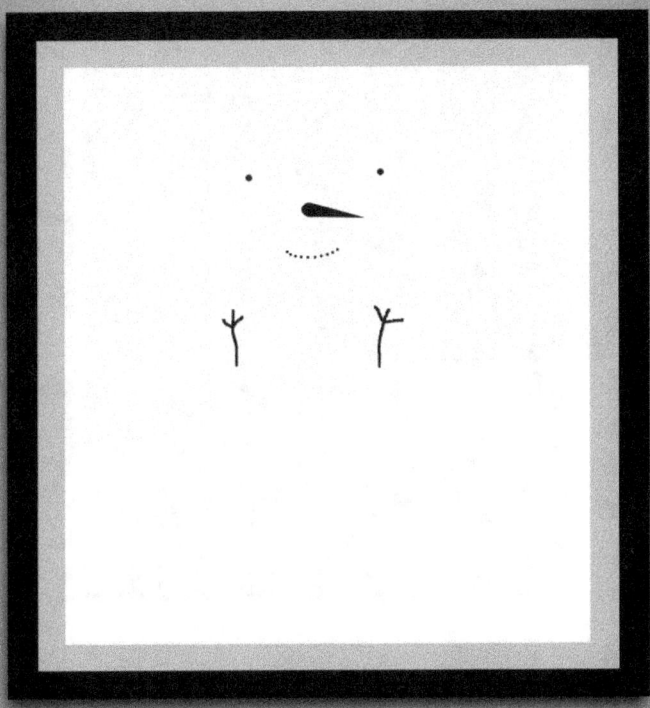

robert melted
"the poem must ride on its
own melting"

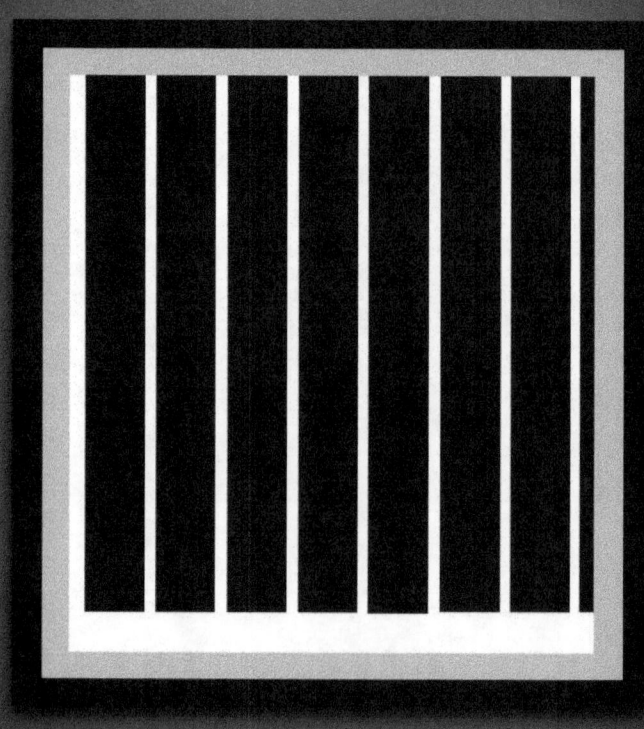

blinds

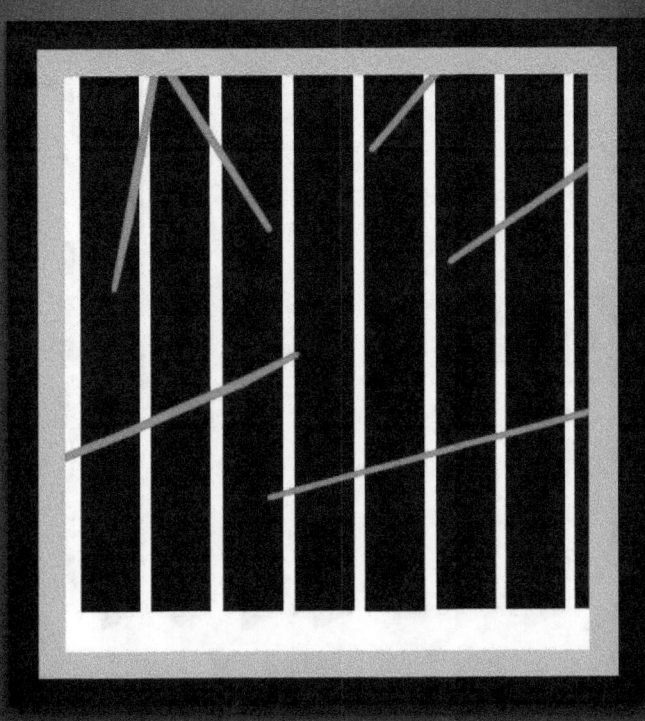

constructive laser surgery

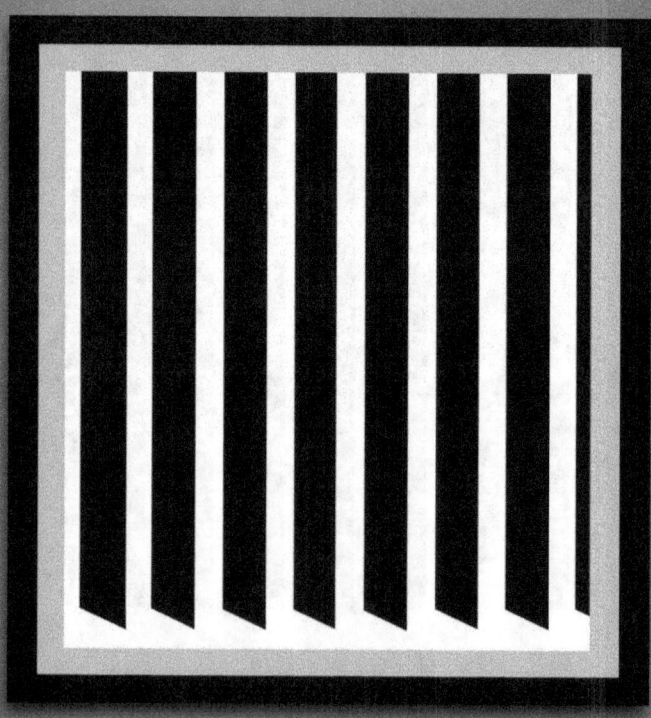

sees

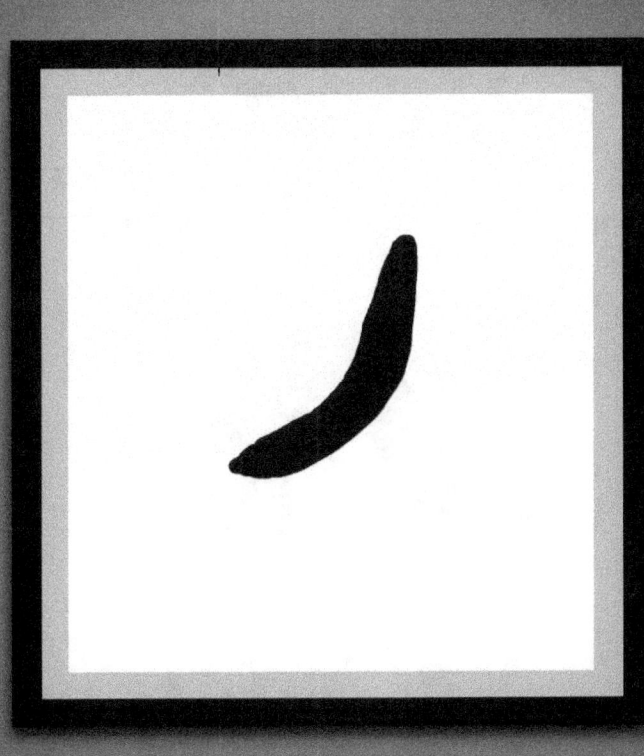

banana

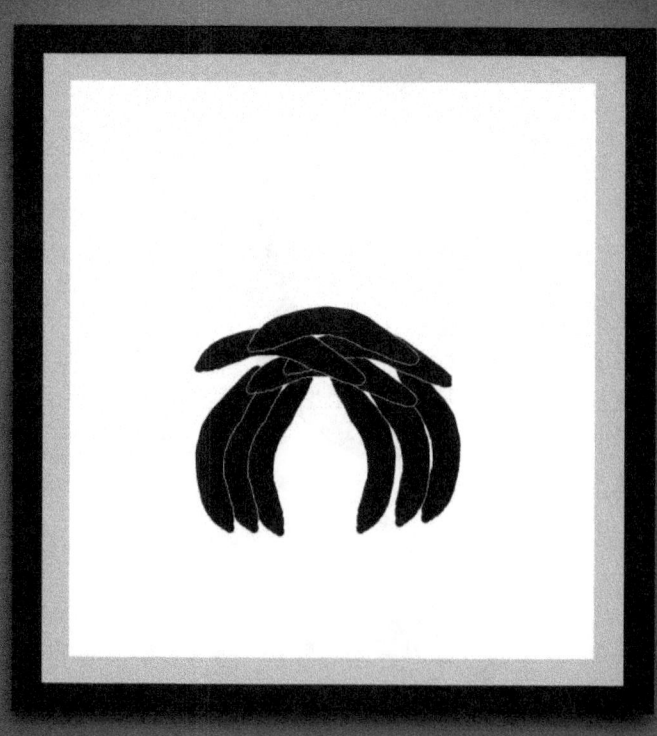

banana spider

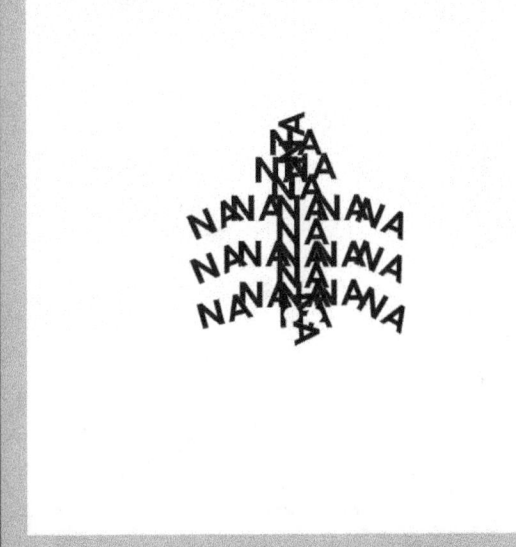

nanana spider

nanana spdr

NA NA Z NNA
NA NANA
NANANA
NA

nanana baetmon

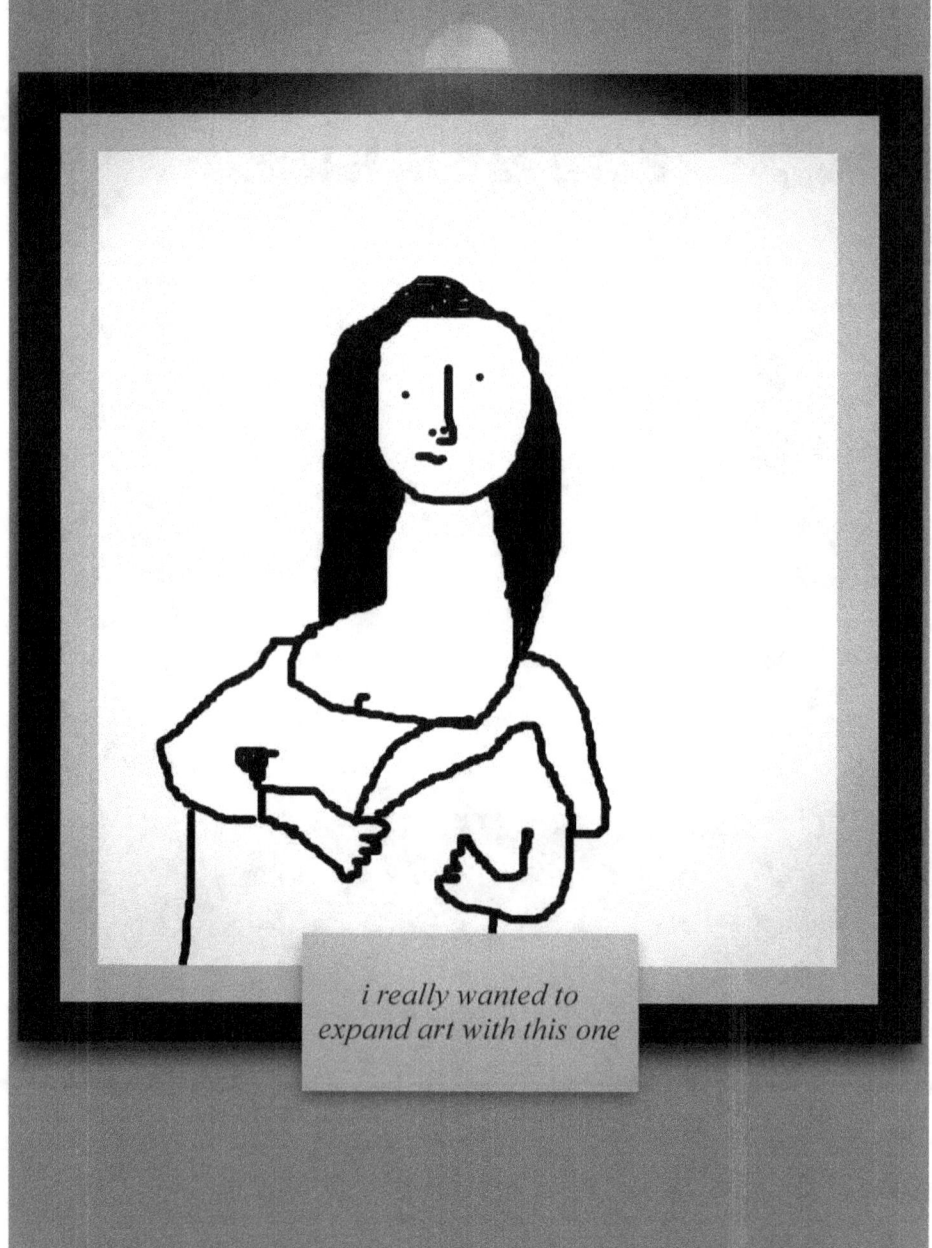

i really wanted to
expand art with this one

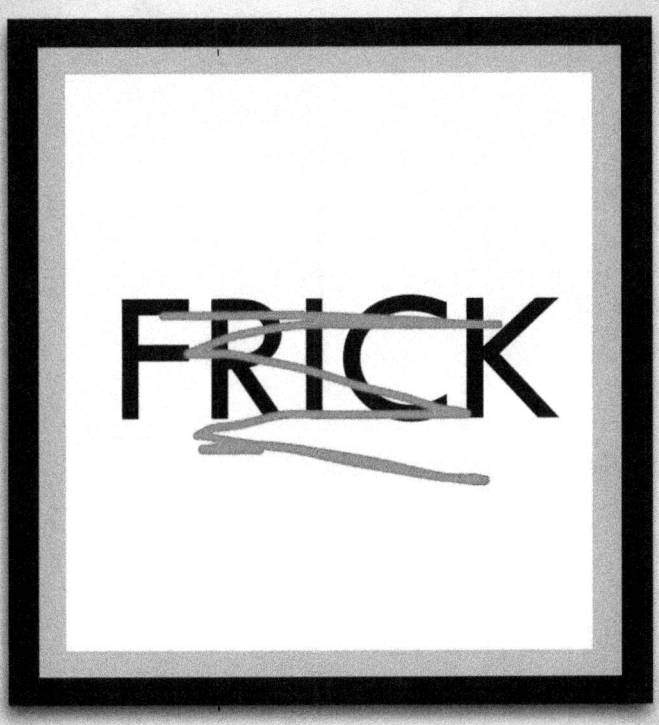

you can't see this word
because censorship,
that's right, thanks trump

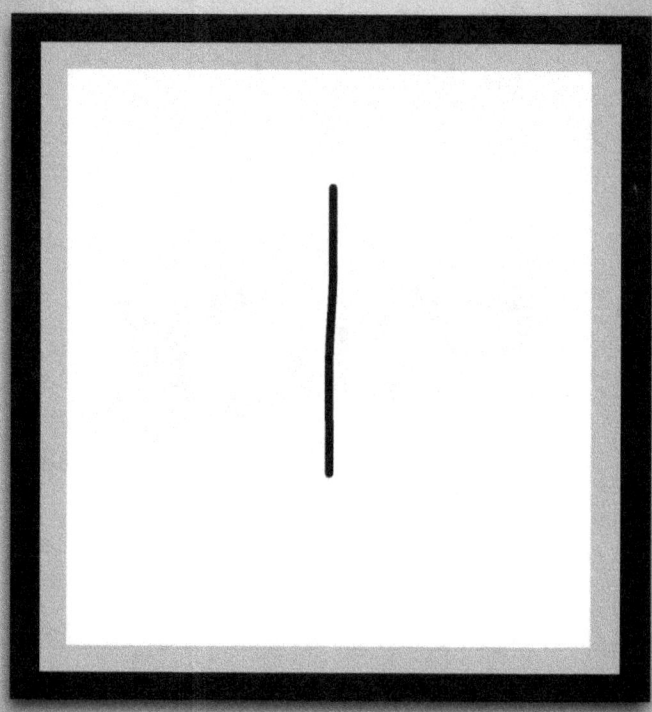

straight line

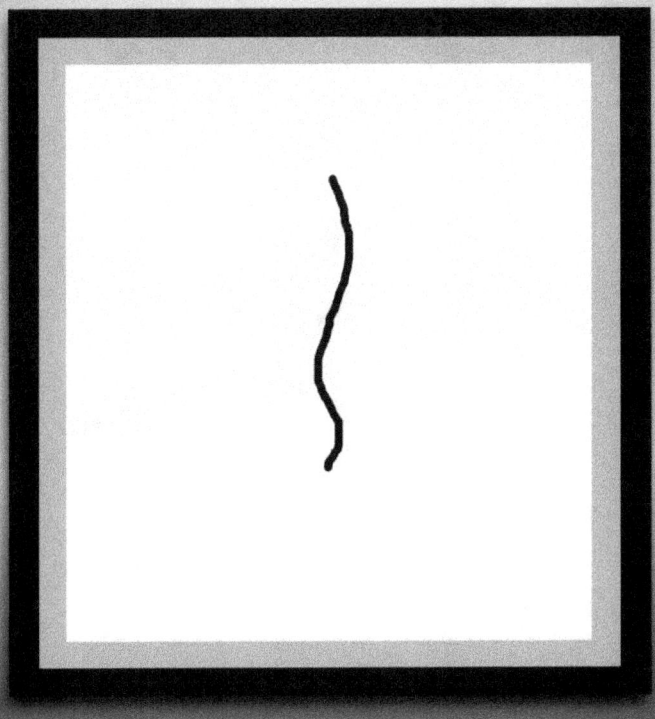

gay line

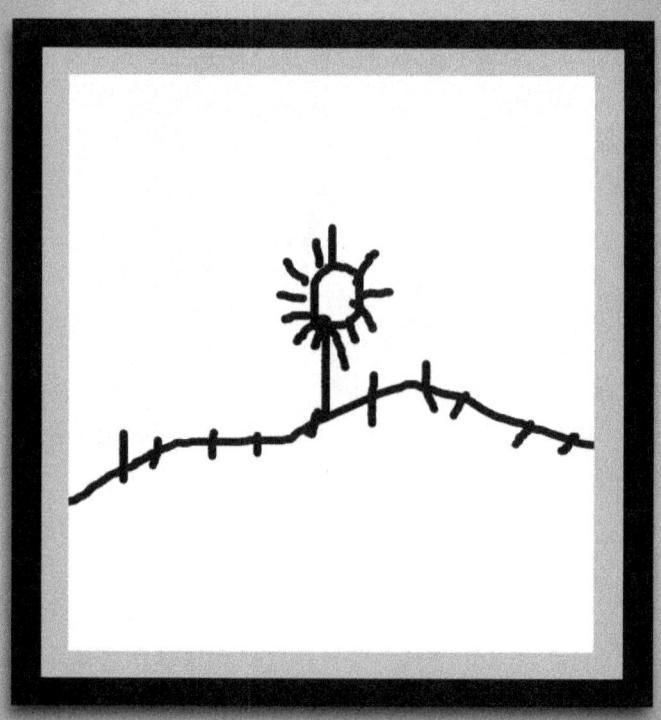

jackson pollock but off lsd

HARRY POTTER IS OVERRATED

true muckraking

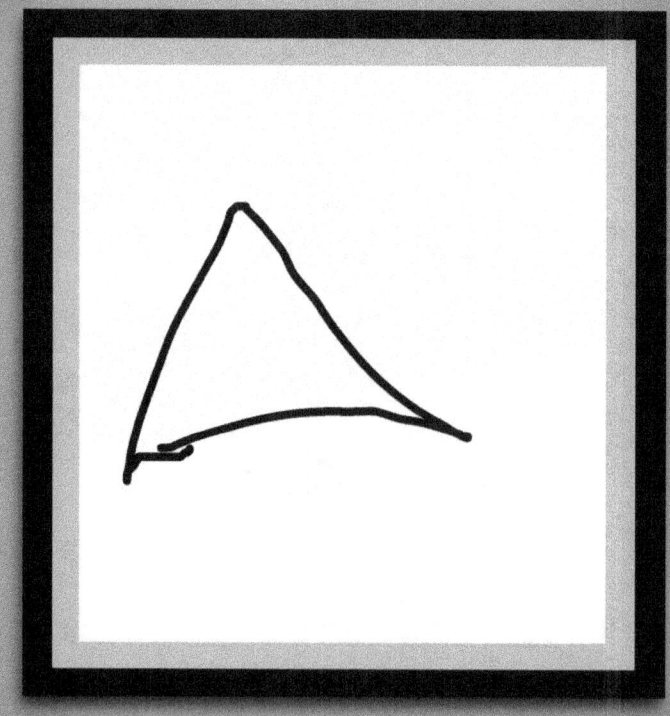

frickin' egyp

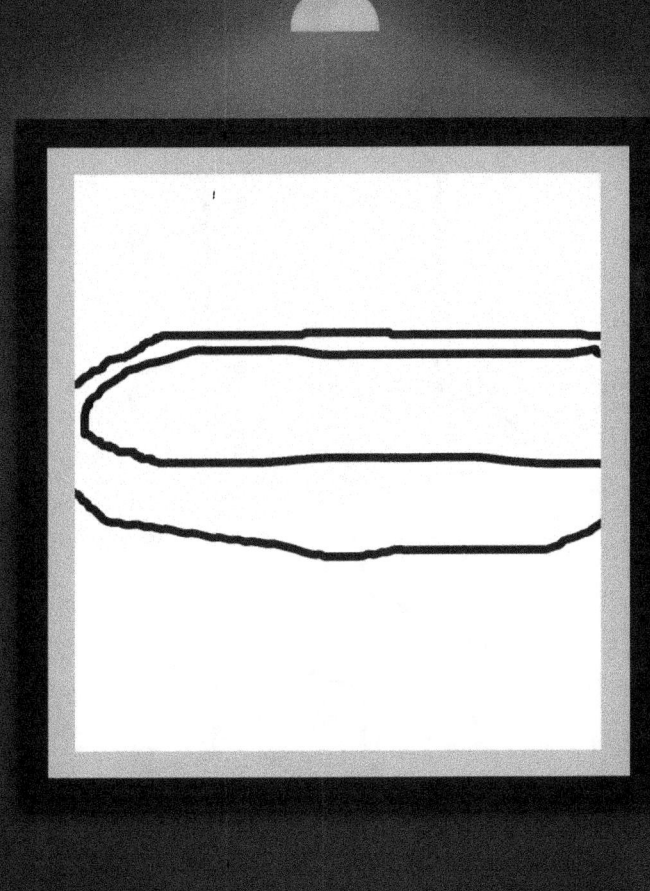

dagum chinya

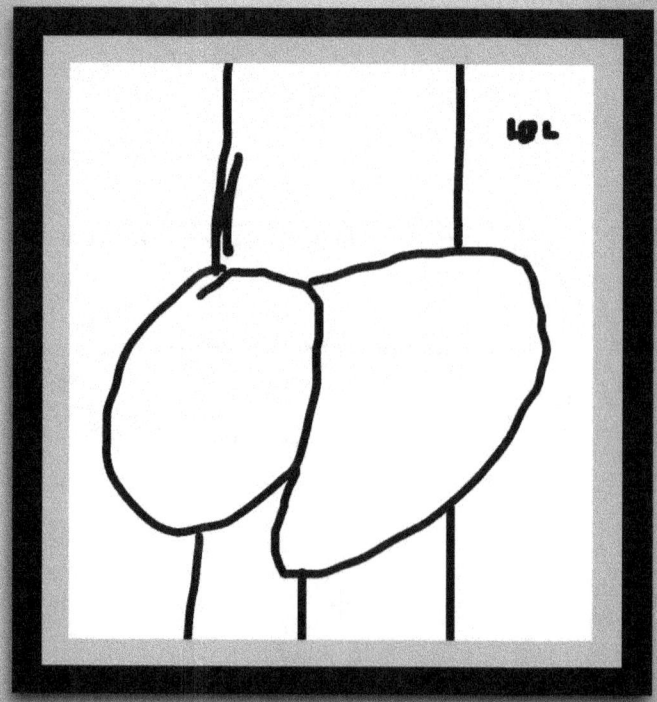

boodha

T GALLERY

introduckshin

i would like to welcome you to the most be
gallery to ever fit in a 6 by 9 inch paperbac

but i'm not with you rn, so i'll have to welc
over this intro page

so *fricking welcome*

over the next 200 pages of absolutely tortu
you're going to feel like you're actually in a
legit art show with all the fancy freaking ri
and deep meanings and weird furniture and

it's all the fun of going to an art showing wi
the judgemental looks from effiminate men
scarves and watermelon martinis

that's right females and gentlemen, now you
the pleasures of art shows without having t
pants

u r there

this art gallery
BOOM inception

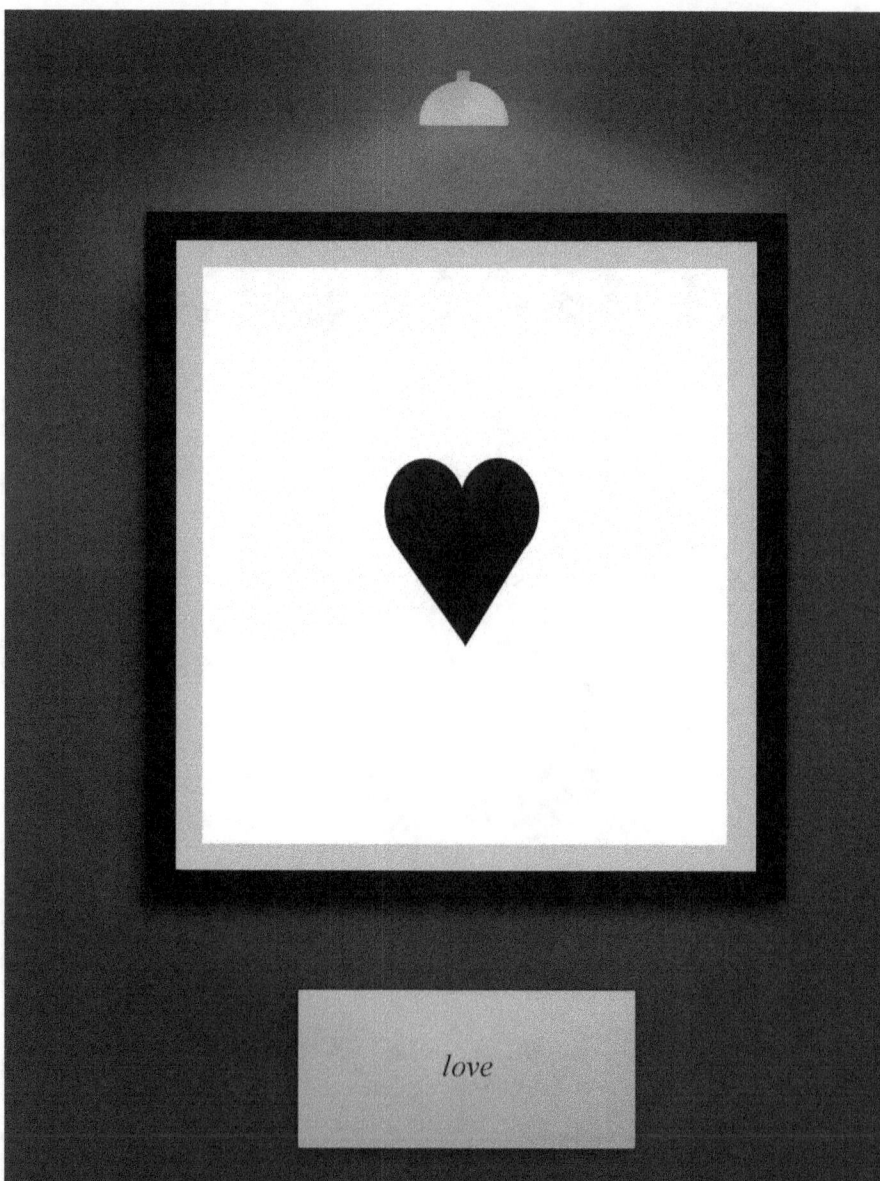

love

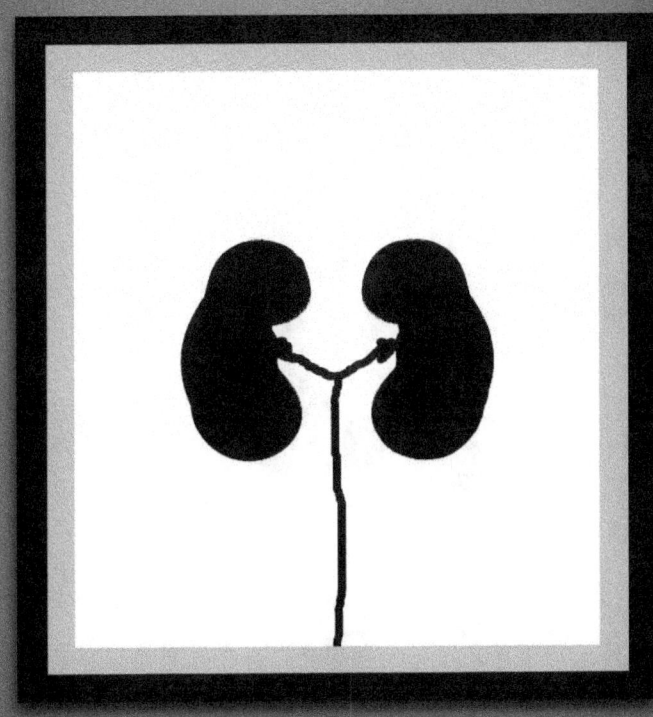

love

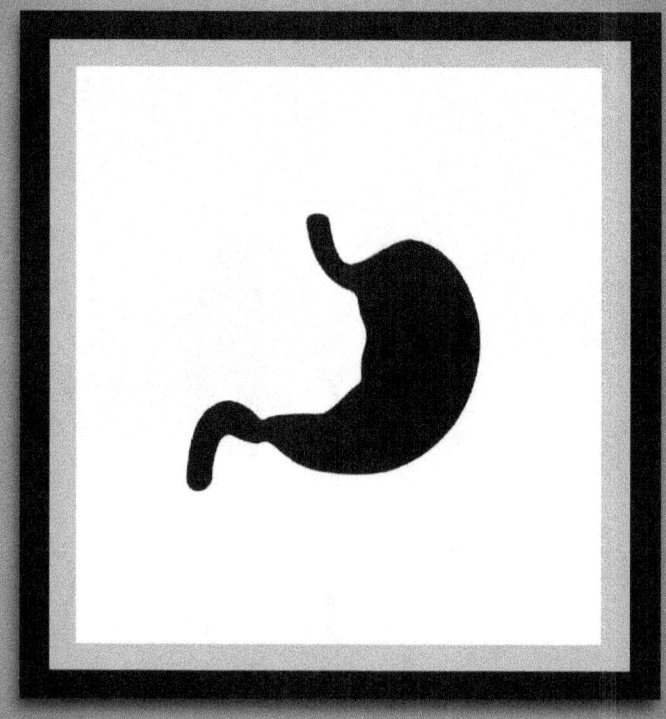

hate

charles the fastidious fish
that's right, don't you
ever be thinking too little
of charles

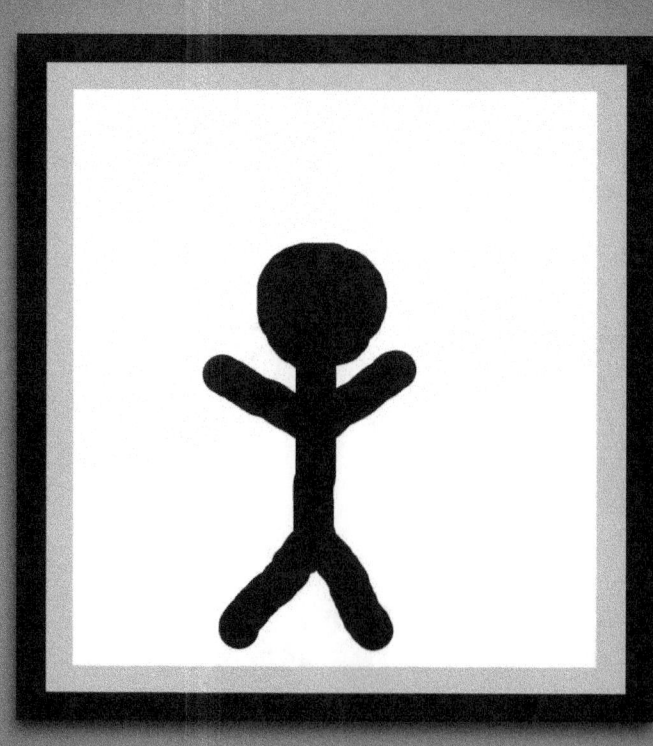

male

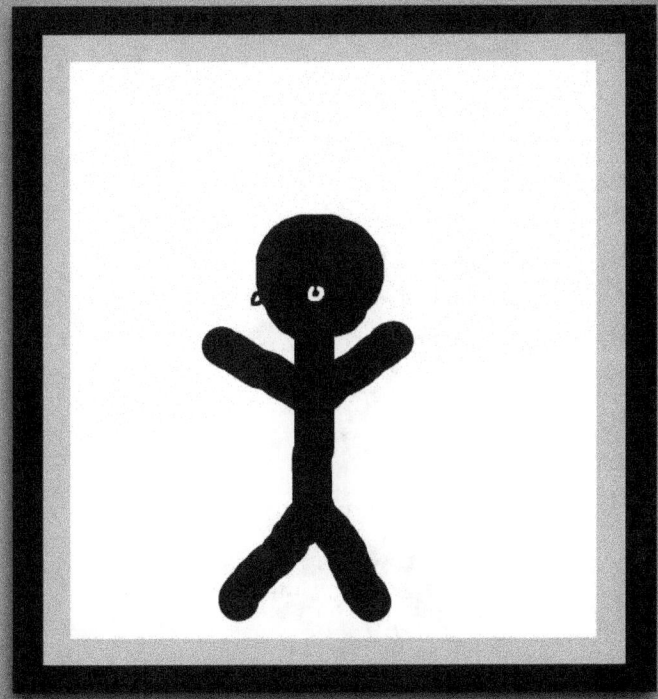

edgy male

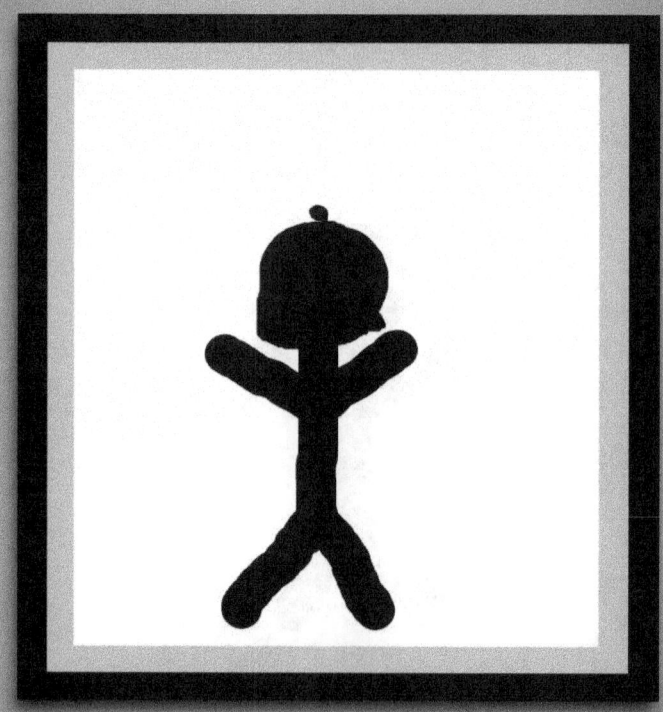

ultra-spiritual male

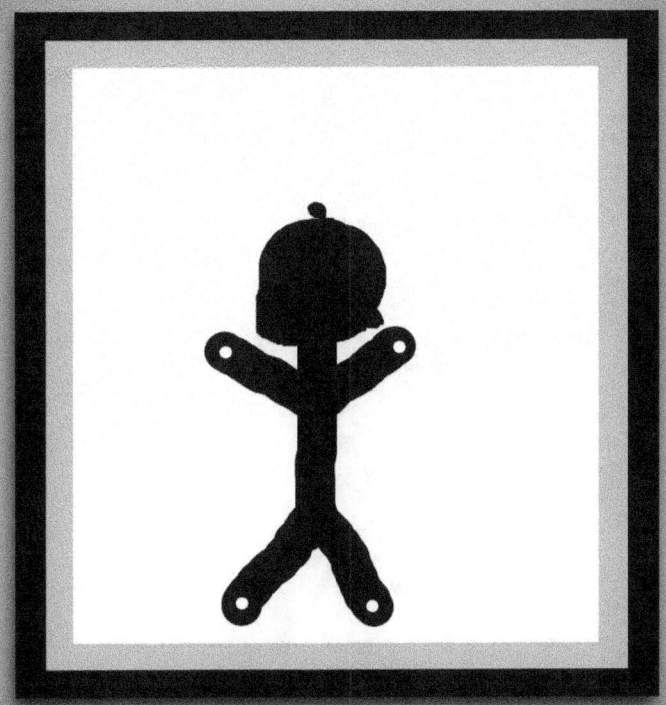

ultra-spiritual male,
special jesus edition

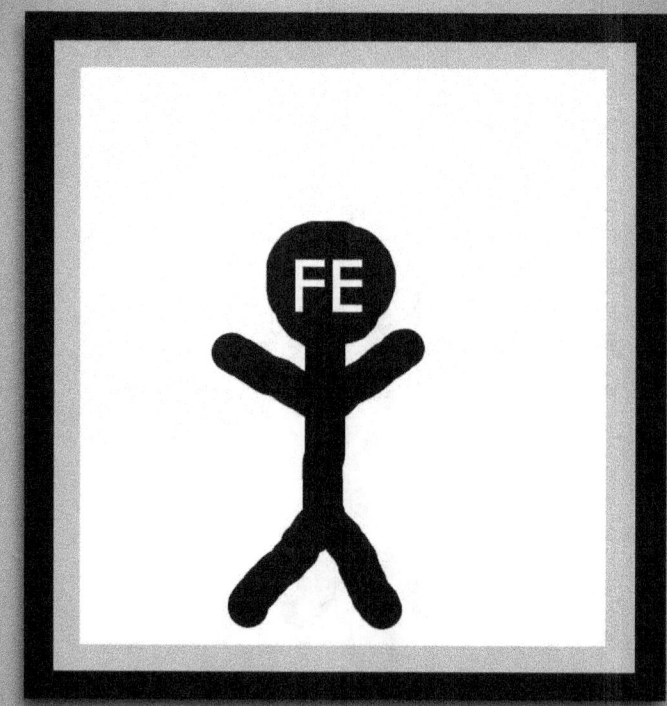

female

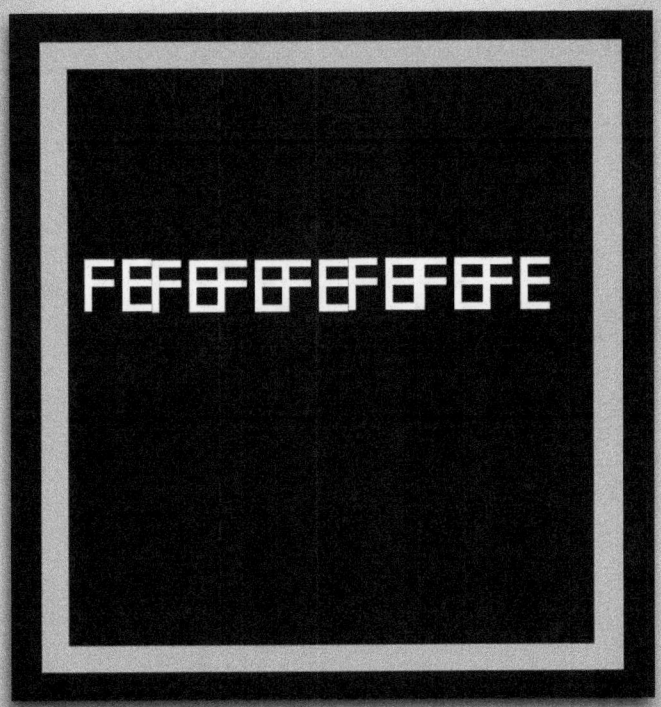

feline

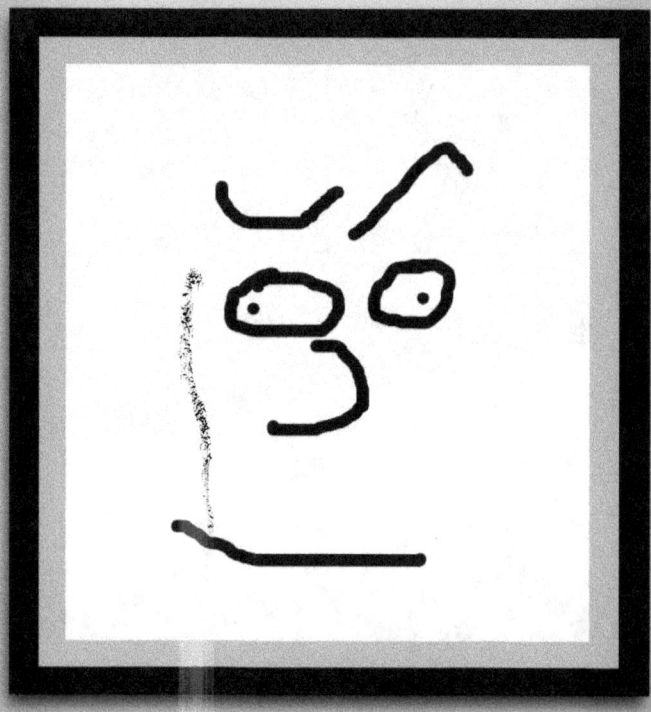

this painting is attracted
to you, sexually

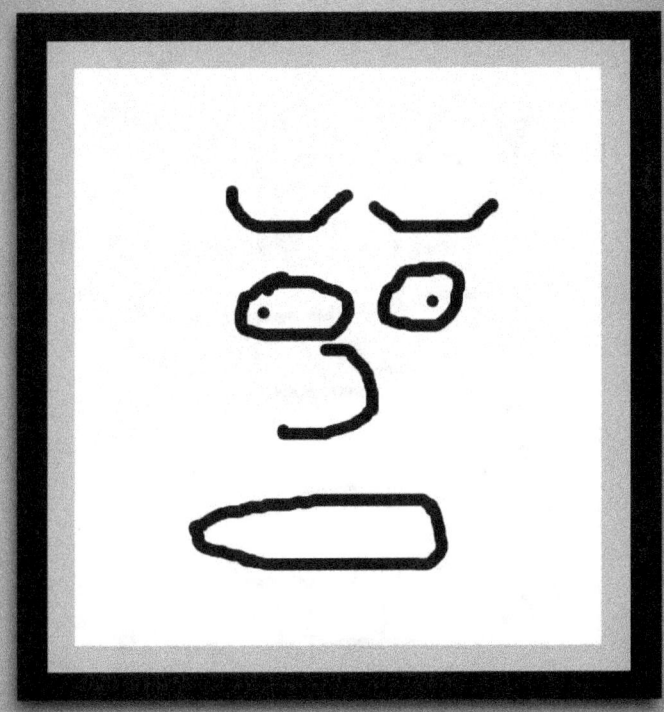

bad painting:
interpaintial marriage is
illegal under statute 420
of the constitution

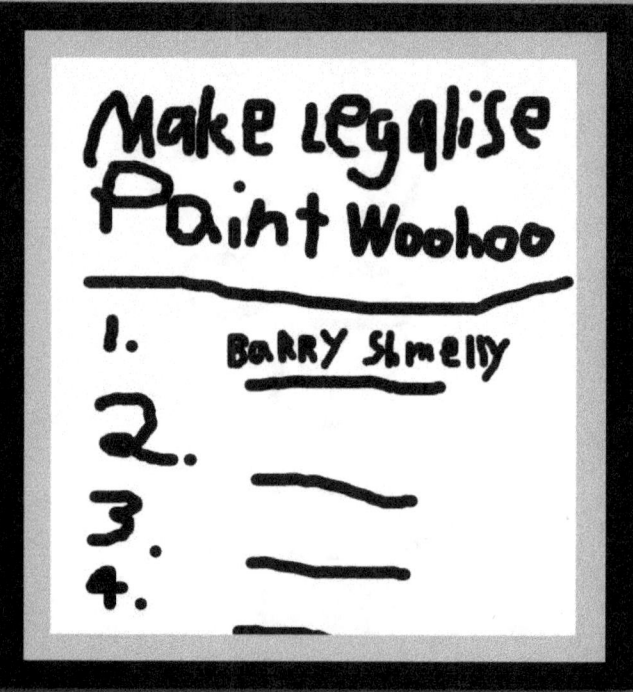

please sign this petition

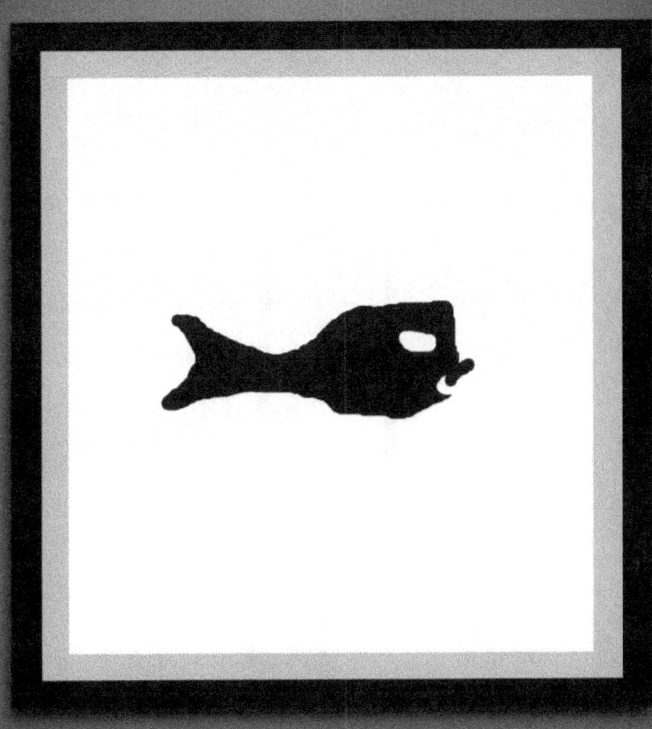

benton the fascist fish...
honestly not a big fan of
this guy

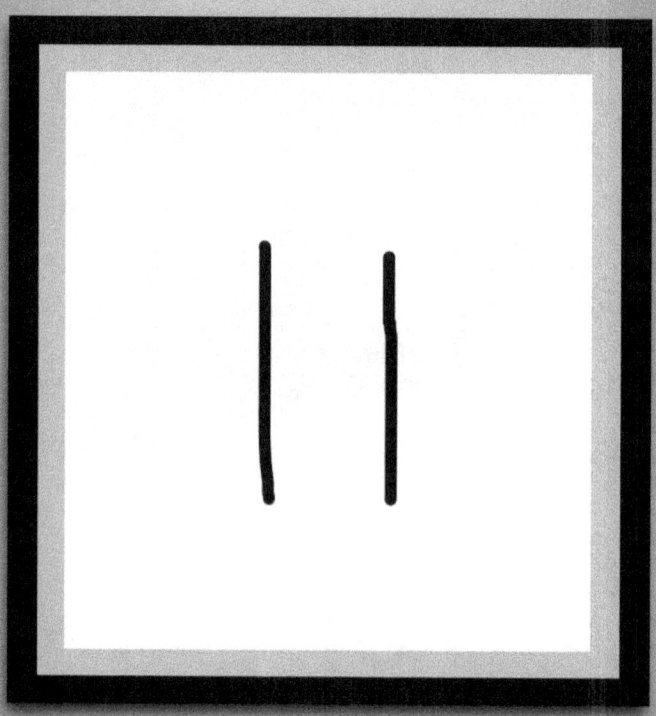

two stick bugs fighting

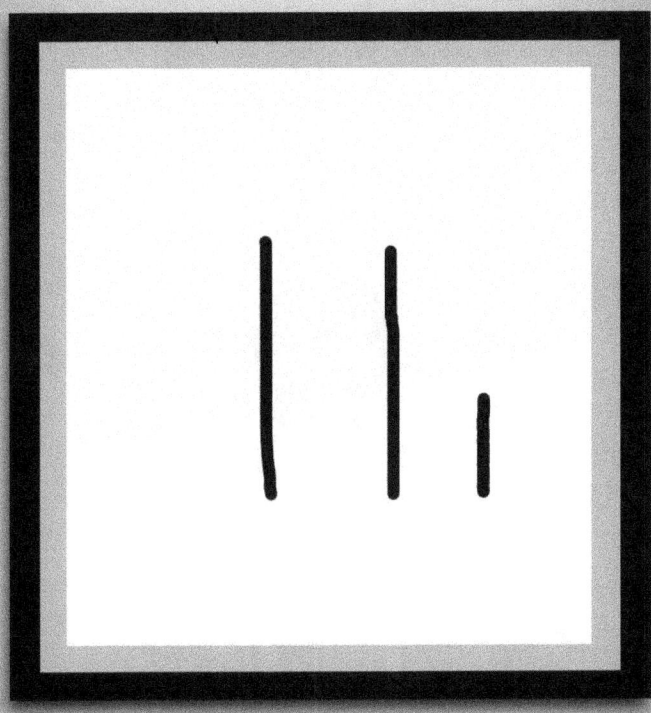

*oh my! now there's a
baby stick*

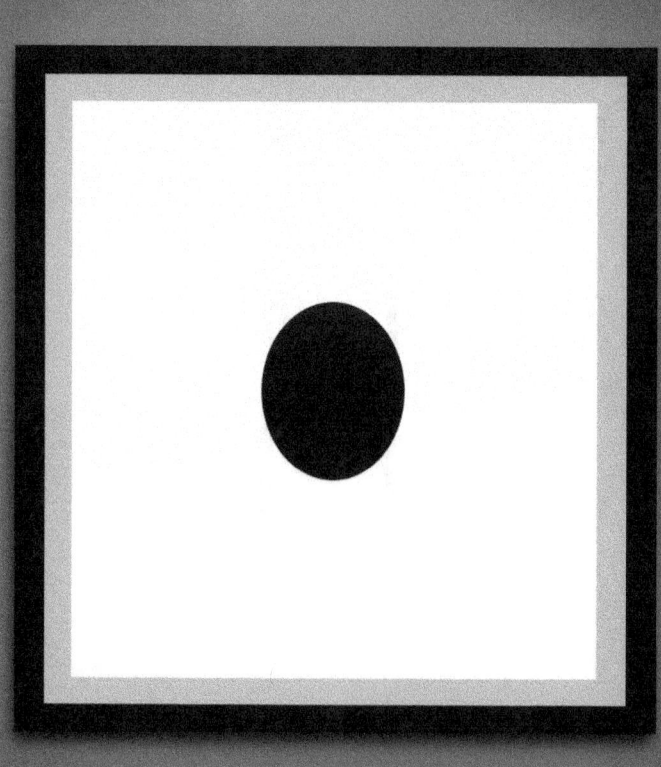

crack it open with your finger bae

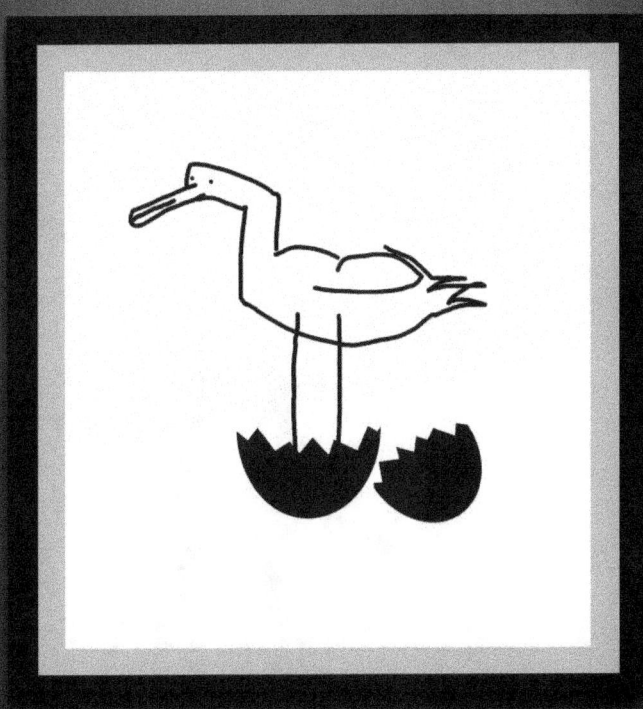

you've done it! and it's,
it's a mongoose!

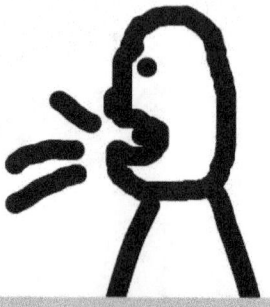

get choke

cpr in three parts:
part one

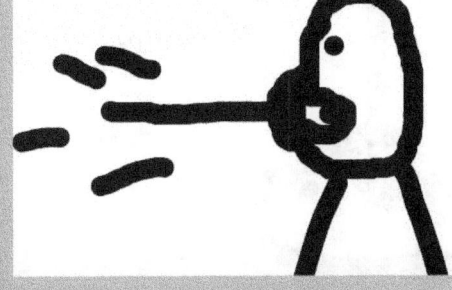

step b

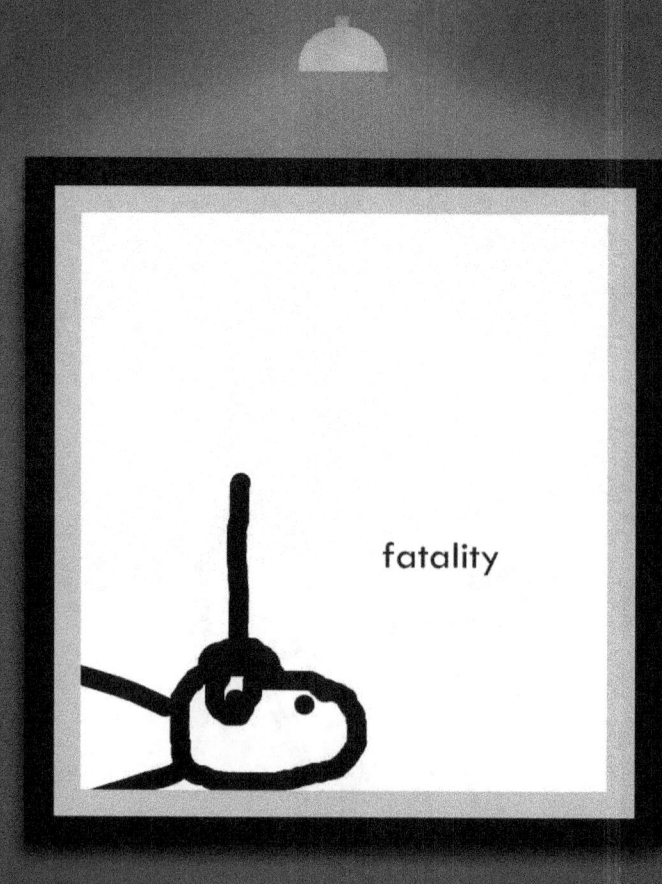

fatality

step 3

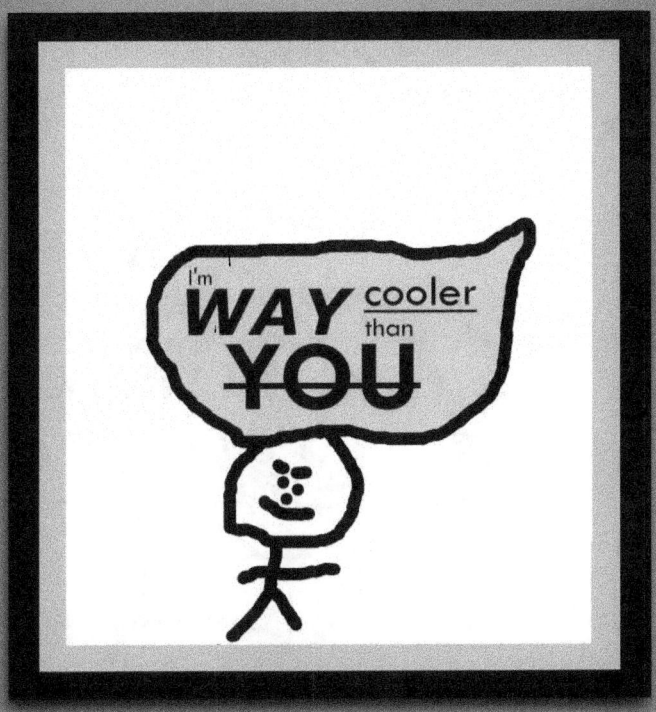

people with orange hair

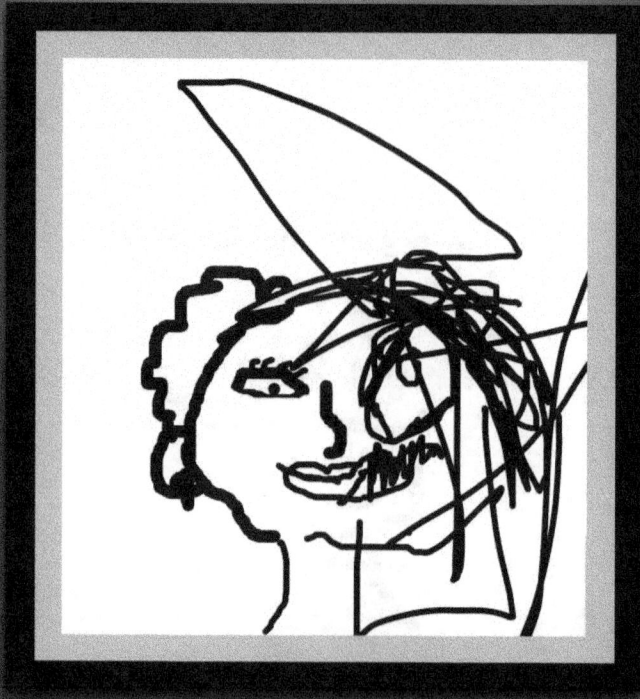

marylin mansonroe

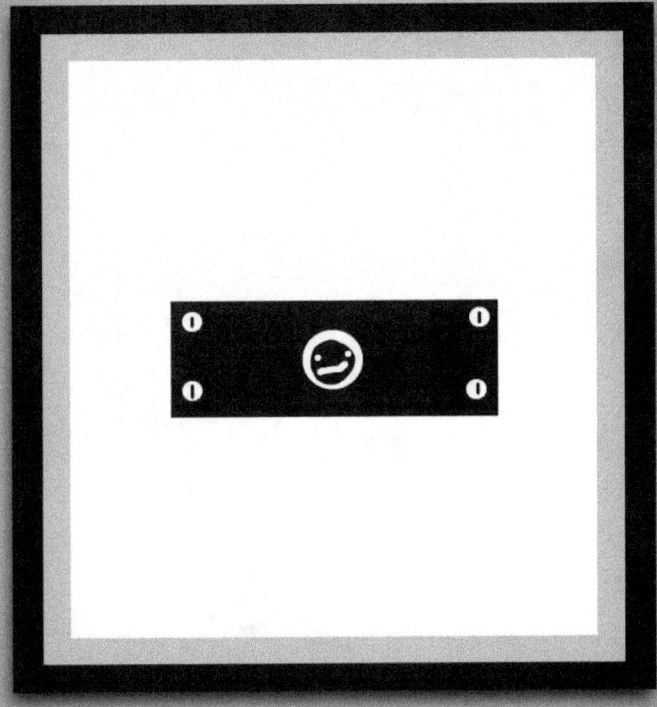

monet

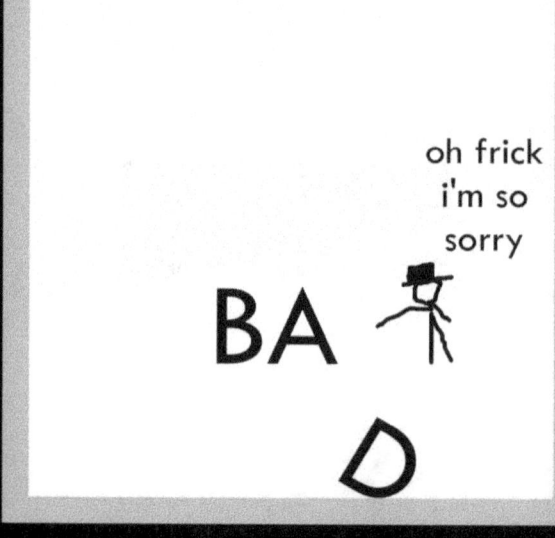

braeking baed

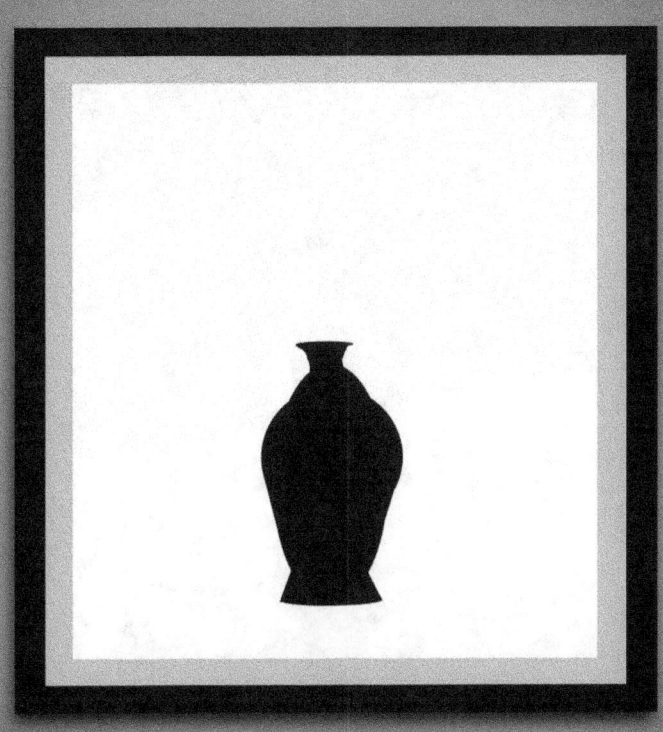

*this is a vozz which is how
rude people say "vase"*

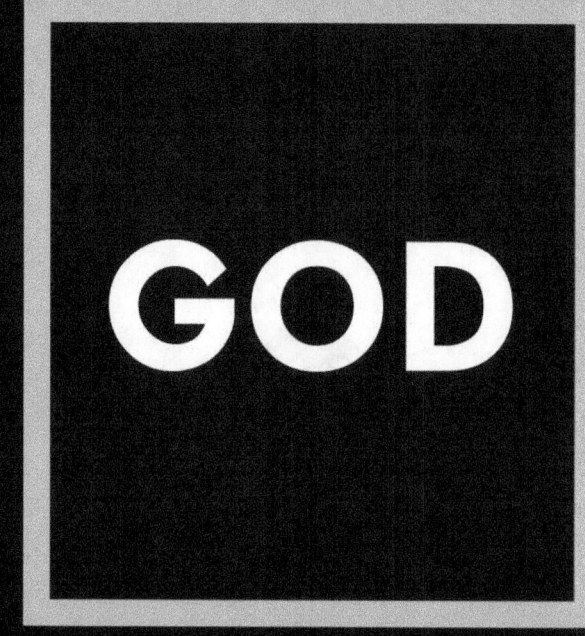

*geez it seems god is white
after all the frick is this*

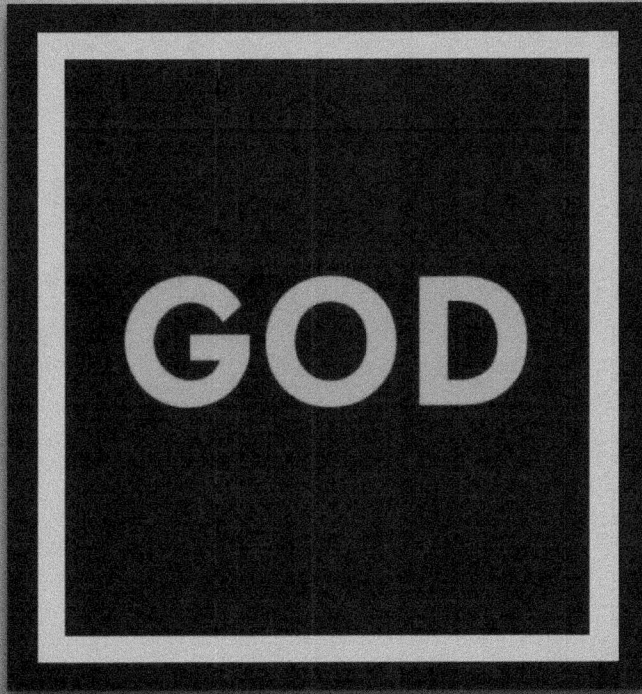

or no he's not, he's a girl

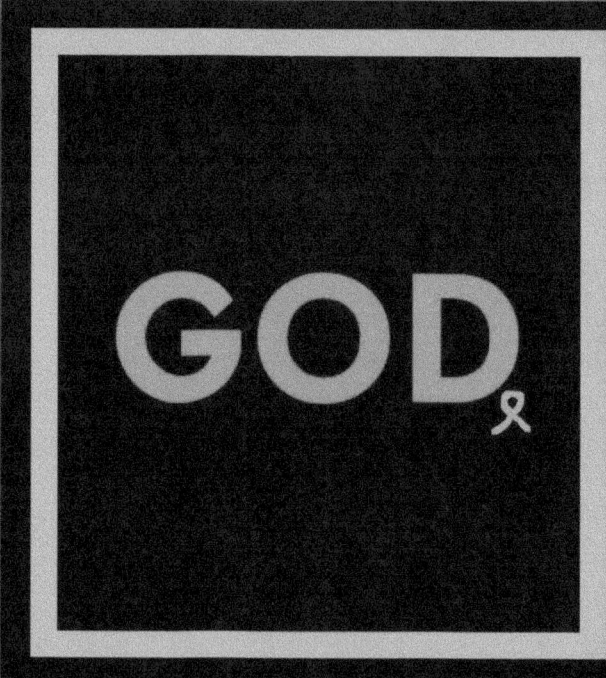

*kidding, he's really just
supporting breast cancer
awareness #thunkpink*

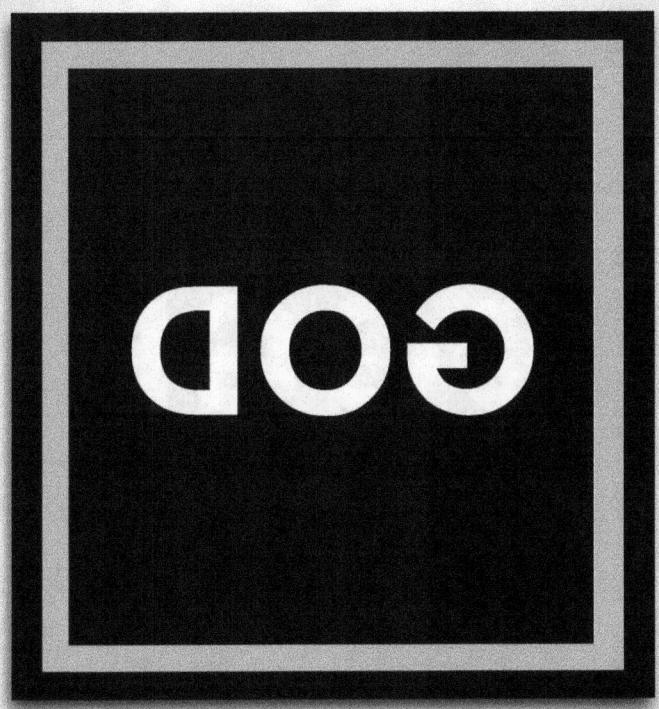

oh frick he must be
confused, woof woof

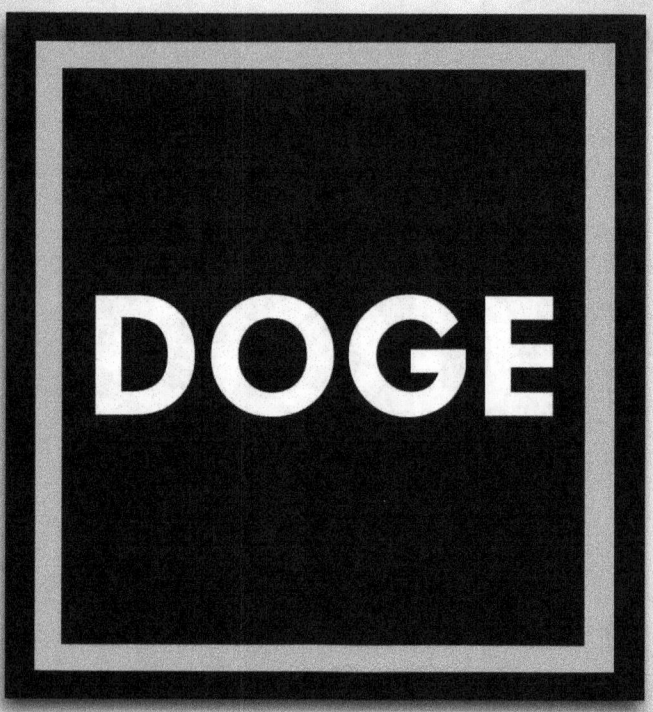

pupper r love, pupper r life

*racially insensitive
drawing*

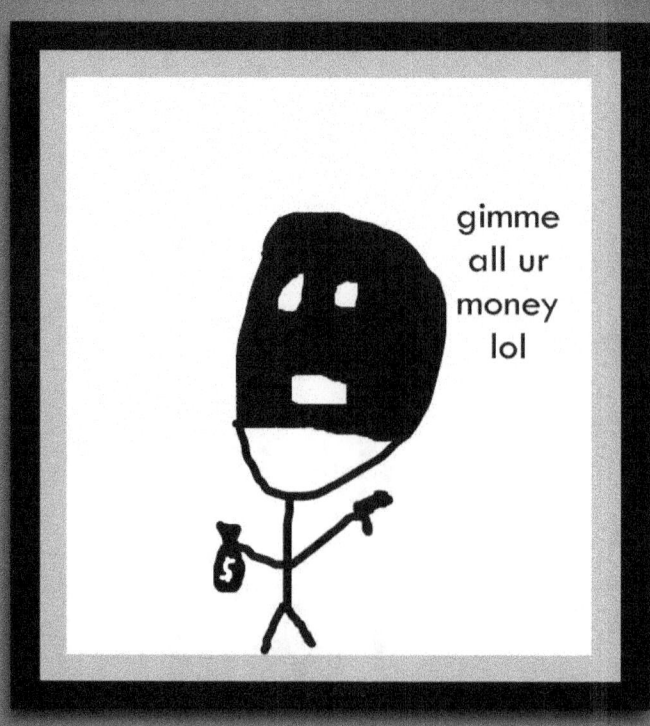

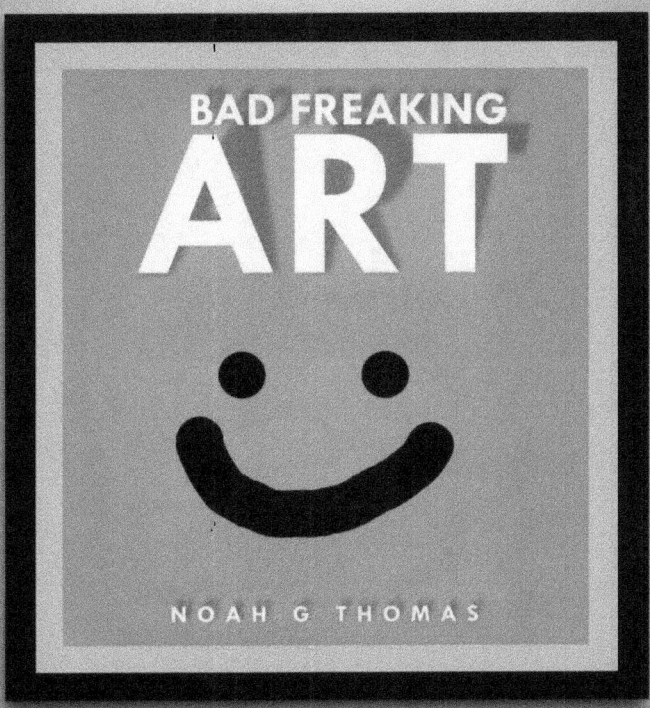

please buy five more copies so i don't need a side job

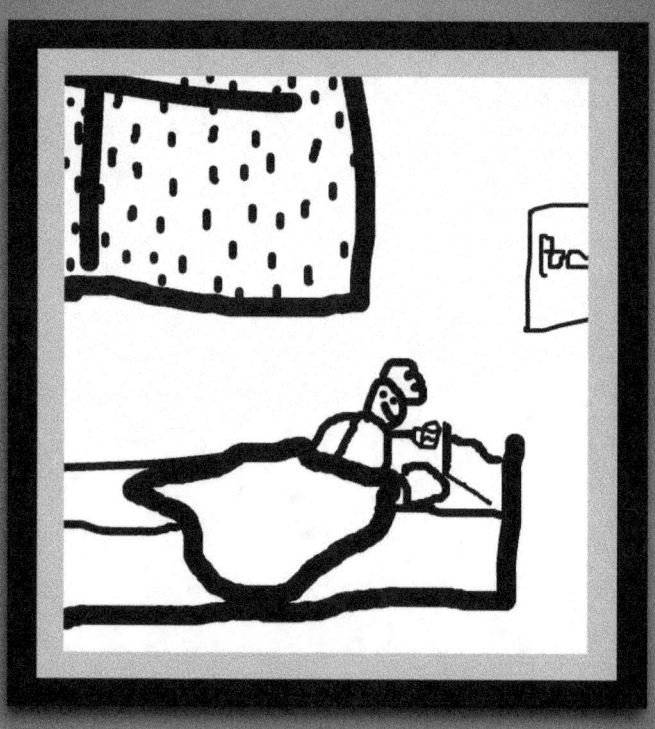

nothin' like snuggling up
on a rainy day with a
happy glass of bleach

HAPPY BIRTHDAY! AND IF IT'S NOT YOUR BIRTHDAY FRICK YOU

congratulations you're 21,
glug glug i mean right?
haha you know it pal
haha go getum ace haha

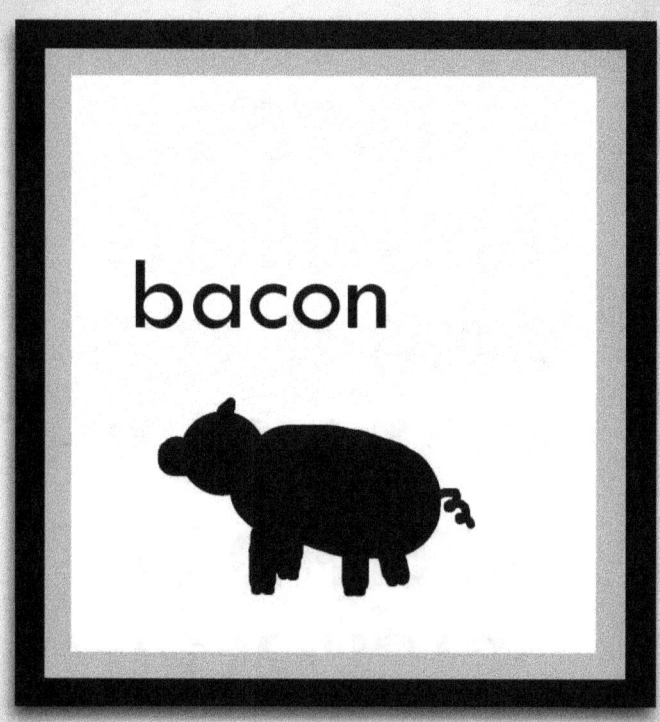

bacon

lol it's funny because of vegans

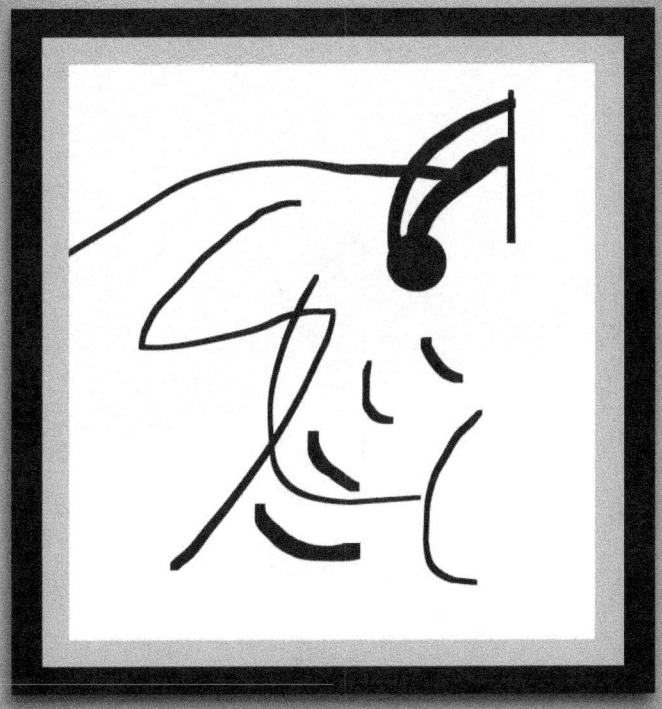

*you may be tempted to try
and find deeper meaning
to this. there's none.
there's not even a joke.*

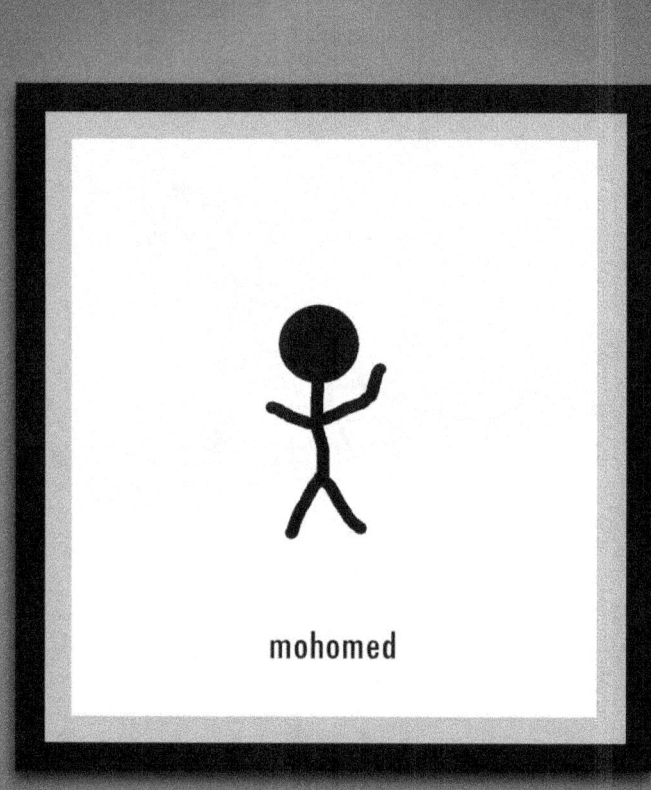

mohomed

pls dont kill me

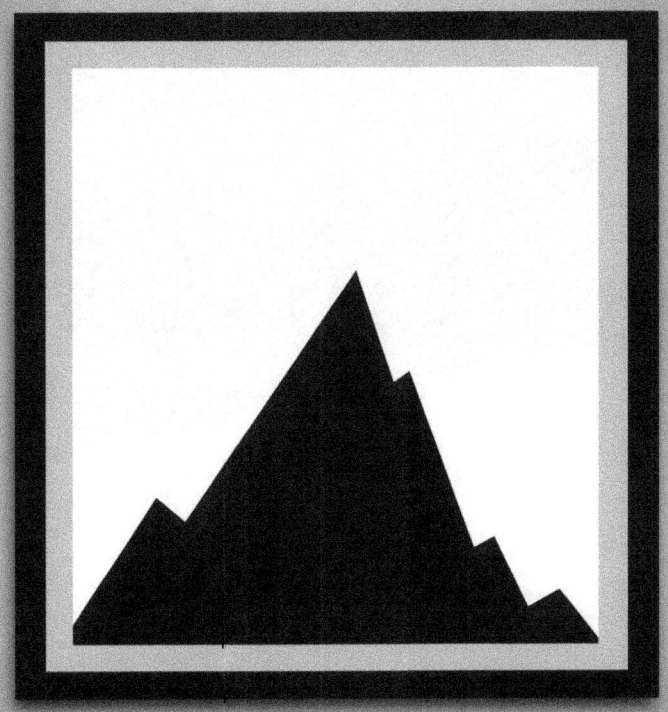

frick boi those are some
frickin bootiful mountains

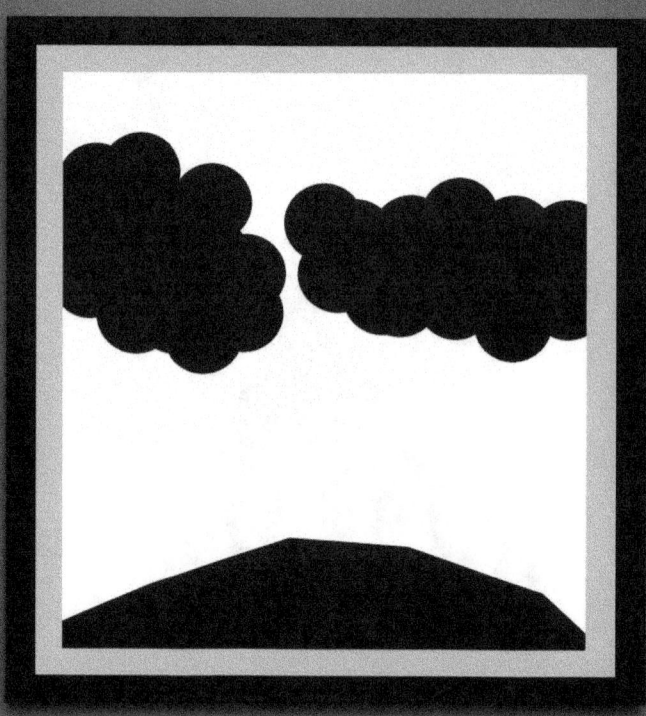

daaang you climbed dat
mountain and you still
thicc

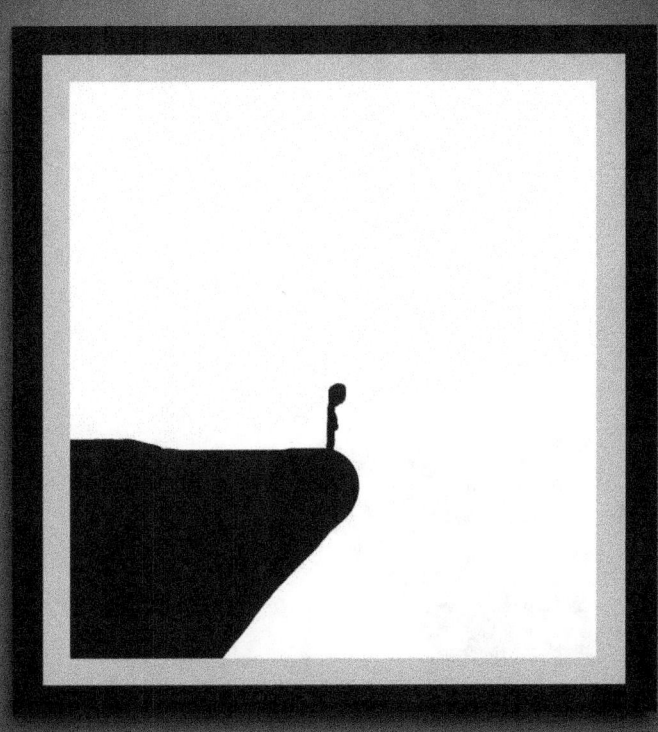

no little dude! there's so much to live for, like this art

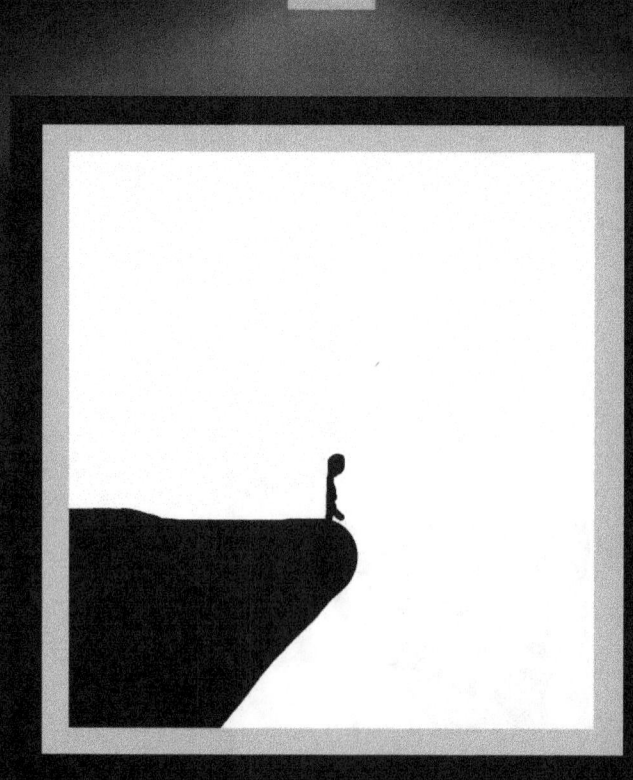

*what? my art... it's...
freaking bad?
i'm sorry.*

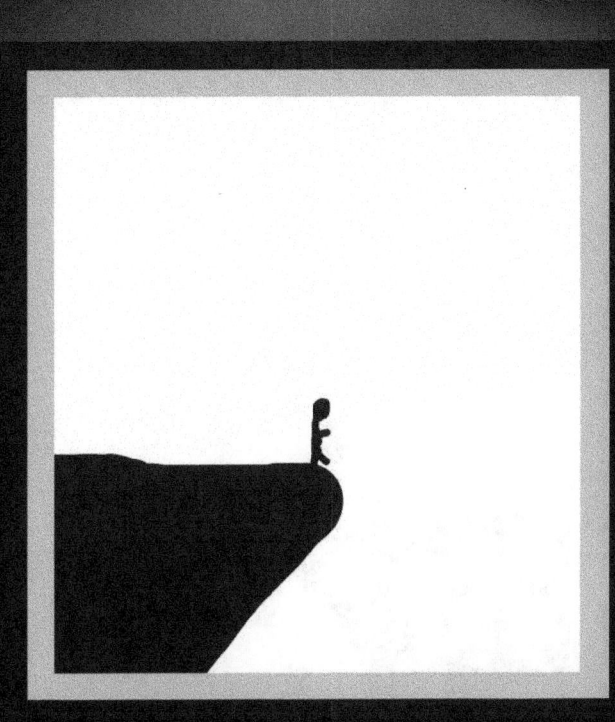

but maybe it's not about
how good it is. maybe
it's good because it
made you laugh

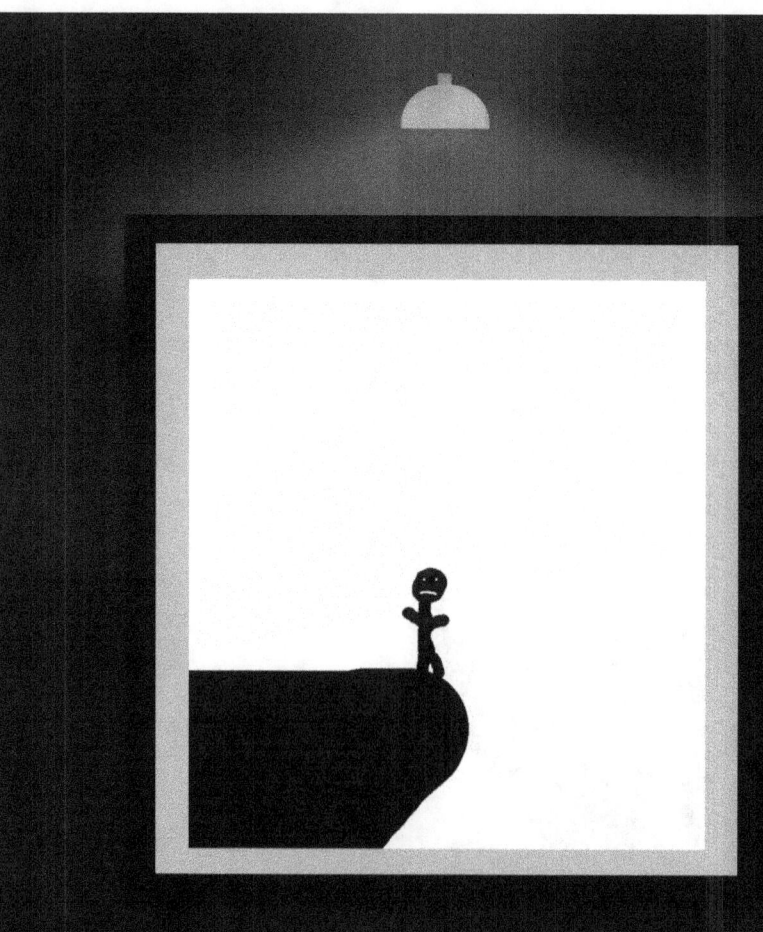

*it's not funny? well just
do it then. do it.*

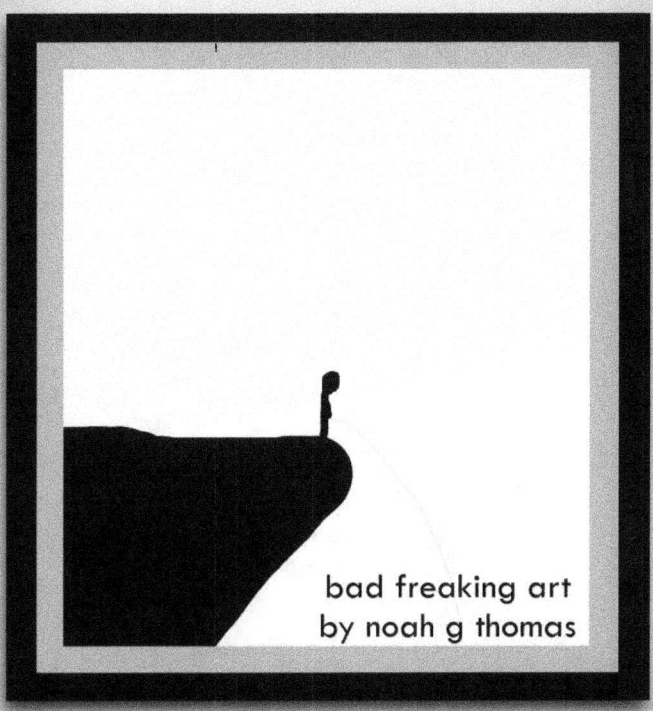

bad freaking art
by noah g thomas

oh... well, frick you
reader personified as
stick man in narrative
metaphor with plot twist

we care about your feelings.
please give this book a review:

(circle one)

not ○ ○ ○ ○ ○ super
                        satisfied

after you're finished please rip this out
and place it inside of your rectum,
where people care about your opinion.

before you go

the end

thank you very much for buying this crappy book
full of bad freaking art

i probably didn't make much money because
colored paper is really expensive. I know, racism
sucks

despite in spite of all this i'd like to have a time
of having some doing some acknowledge mints

i'd like to thank myself for making this crap,
thank god for making me, and thank all you
guys for absolute frickin nothing. indeed without
all of you this all would have still happened

but really you spent like 15 dollars or something
you really should've donated that to charity or
something useful so thanks

k love you honey I'm gonna let you go now bi

this is the last page
obviously